Enchantment of the World

YUGOSLAVIA

By Carol Greene

Consultant: David MacKenzie, Ph.D., University of North Carolina, Greensboro, North Carolina

Consultant for Reading: Robert L. Hillerich, Ph.D., Bowling Green State University, Bowling Green, Ohio

CHILDRENS PRESS, CHICAGO

Shopping at an outdoor market in Rovinj

This book is for Vojislav Kostić, with thanks for his generosity and hospitality, and for Gragotin Cvetko, with thanks for his wisdom and kindness.

Picture Acknowledgments
Root Resources: ©J. William Langill: 4, 14, 32 (left); ©Leonard Gordon: 5, 13; ©Mary Langill: 6, 16, 35 (left), 37, 64; ©Jane P. Downton: 101 (left); ©Irene E. Hubbell: 8 (left), 26 (right), 31, 59 (right), 61, 101 (right); ©Byron Crader: Cover, 9, 42, 46, 93 (2 photos), 97; ©Lloyd Haugen: 12, 17, 33 (right), 54, 76, 90, 92
Hillstrom Stock Photos: ©Jim Ferri: 8 (right), 22, 26 (left), 34, 39, 103 (bottom); ©Martha L. Crump: 56 (left), 59 (left)
Colour Library International: 10, 20, 35 (right), 36, 58 (bottom), 62, 63
Renee Neiberg: 15
Yugoslav Press and Cultural Center, New York City: 18, 19, 21, 24, 28, 41, 44, 45, 50, 56 (right), 70, 71, 81 (top and bottom left), 85 (right), 86 (2 photos), 88 (2 photos), 89 (2 photos), 94 (2 photos), 95, 96 (left), 98, 102, 103 (top), 117, 119
A.F. Kersting, Architectural Photographer: 27, 33 (left)
Gladys J. Peterson: 32 (right), 58 (top), 81 (bottom right), 84, 91, 96 (right), 100
Historical Pictures Service, Chicago: 49, 52 (2 photos), 53, 66 (2 photos), 67, 69
United Press International: 72, 85 (left)
Wide World Photos: 83
James P. Rowan: 79
Len Meents: Map on pages 15, 24, 29, 30, 34, 36, 39, 41, 43, 67
Courtesy Flag Research Center, Winchester, Massachusetts 01890: Flag on back cover
Cover: The Mostar Bridge over the Neretva River

Library of Congress Cataloging in Publication Data

Greene, Carol.
    Yugoslavia.

    (Enchantment of the world)
    Includes index.
    Summary: An introduction to the geography, history, government, culture, and people of the six diverse republics that make up the southern European country of Yugoslavia.
    1. Yugoslavia—Juvenile literature. [1. Yugoslavia]
I. Title. II. Series.
DR1214.G73   1984   949.7   83-21049
ISBN 0-516-02791-3   AACR2

Budva, a popular seaside resort in Montenegro

TABLE OF CONTENTS

Muslim women shopping in Sarajevo

Chapter 1

A GLORIOUS

COMBINATION

Take three official languages—Serbo-Croation, Slovenian, and Macedonian. Throw in several other languages, too—such as Hungarian, Italian, and Albanian—and many different dialects (ways of speaking the same language). Now take two official alphabets—Cyrillic and Roman. Take three major religions—Orthodox, Roman Catholic, and Muslim—plus some smaller ones. Take four nationalities—Serb, Croat, Slovene, and Macedonian. Add several more nationalities in small quantities. Put all these together into six republics and two provinces and what do you have? The nation known as Yugoslavia. You also have a glorious combination.

SO MUCH TO ENJOY

In Yugoslavia there are old stone buildings with red tile roofs and new skyscrapers of concrete and glass. A gleaming modern bus stops in the middle of a mountain road while shepherds lead

Workers fix tile on a roof (left). Sheep are raised in the mountainous areas and are used for producing meat, milk, and wool.

their sheep from one side to the other. There are stones that look like flowers and flowers carved from stone.

There are other kinds of stones, too—tombstones with simple pictures of soldiers carved on them. In the pictures, these soldiers, complete with twirled mustaches, stand proudly at attention. But no one lies beneath the stones. The soldiers were buried on some distant battlefields. People in their home villages put the stones along the roadside so the fallen loved ones would not be forgotten. It's important to remember that the Yugoslav people have had a long and bloody history.

SOUNDS, AND MORE

What of the sounds of Yugoslavia? The crash of a mountain waterfall, hurtling over hundreds of feet of bare rock, shatters the silence. The cry of a muezzin, calling the Muslim faithful to prayer, echoes across rooftops. Trains on the recently completed

A waterfall in Sibenik

Belgrade-Bar railway roar across the country. (They go through 253 tunnels on the way.) The soft whine of a gypsy's violin serenades diners in a tiny café.

At a small hotel in eastern Serbia one might suddenly hear a low, moaning sound. Is it really just the wind blowing through the trees? There are stories about vampires in eastern Serbia. Could it be?

Back in Belgrade, squeaky voices entertain at the Little Theater. The voices belong to puppets performing a play written by children for children.

In the Macedonian mountains šarplaninac dogs can be heard barking. They are a local breed of sheep dog that has been helping Macedonian shepherds for centuries. It is said that one of these dogs can fight several wolves at once—and win. A team of only two dogs can care for as many as two thousand sheep. No wonder the shepherds love them!

These are some of the sights and sounds that make up the glorious combination of this amazingly varied nation. But there is more ahead in Yugoslavia. Much, much more.

A wood-tiled chalet in the mountains of Slovenia.

Chapter 2

A MIXTURE OF TERRAINS

NEIGHBORS AND REPUBLICS

Yugoslavia lies on a big wedge of land known as the Balkan
Peninsula. Her neighbors are Italy to the west, Austria and
Hungary to the north, Rumania and Bulgaria to the east, and
Greece and Albania to the south. Yugoslavia's location right in the
midst of so many other countries has had much to do with her
long, bloody history.

Yugoslavia's territory covers 98,766 square miles (255,804
square kilometers). That makes her a little larger than Wyoming
or West Germany and a little smaller than Italy or New Zealand.

Politically, Yugoslavia is divided into six republics: Serbia,
Croatia, Bosnia-Hercegovina, Slovenia, Macedonia, and
Montenegro. There are also two self-governing provinces:
Vojvodina and Kosovo-Metohija, both located in Serbia. The
political divisions match the different kinds of Slavic people living
in each area. But Yugoslavia falls into three sections
geographically.

The Coastal Region is rocky and mountainous.

ROCKS AND ROSES

To the west is the Coastal Region, a narrow strip that runs along the Adriatic Sea. Parts of Slovenia, Croatia, and Montenegro lie in the Coastal Region. It also includes about six hundred islands in the sea itself. These islands are the tops of a mountain range that long ago sank into the sea.

Like much of Yugoslavia, the Coastal Region is rocky and mountainous. In many places, sheer cliffs jut straight up out of the sea and fold into range after range of inland mountains. Much of the rock is a special kind of limestone called karst.

An old Slovenian legend tells how the Coastal Region land got so stony. It seems that God had finally finished creating the huge, glorious Alps to the north and found he had a big sack of rocks left over. He was heading south, carrying the sack, when suddenly it split open. Rocks showered down over the Coastal Region and there they have remained to this day.

But, says the legend, God didn't leave the area entirely to rocks. He discovered a rose in the bottom of the sack. So he planted it in a bay at the edge of the sea. The rose took root and soon the little

Portorož, the Harbor of Roses

bay was filled with flowers. They gave the town that grew up there its name—Portorož, or Harbor of Roses.

The town of Portorož still exists and is a favorite spot for vacationers. In fact, millions of tourists (both foreign and Yugoslavian) flock to the Coastal Region each year to enjoy the sunny beaches and beautiful scenery. Tourism provides jobs for many people in this area. The Adriatic Sea provides jobs for others. Fishing boats of all sizes put out from the many bays that line the Coastal Region.

ROCKS AND MORE ROCKS

Inland from the Coastal Region lie the Interior Highlands. This is the largest geographical area of Yugoslavia and is almost all mountains. In the northwest section tower the Julian Alps, a winter paradise for skiers. One of the peaks, Mount Triglav, rises 9,393 feet (2,863 meters) into the air. It is the highest point in Yugoslavia.

Vrsic Pass in the Alps near the Italian border

The Dinaric Alps run parallel to the Coastal Region down the entire length of Yugoslavia and curve into Greece, Bulgaria, and Rumania. In many ways they're like a mighty stone wall. Over the centuries they've helped keep some invaders out of Yugoslavia and made it difficult for others to intrude very far. But they've given the Yugoslavs some headaches, too. Building roads and laying railroad track through all that rock hasn't been easy.

Like the rock in the Coastal Region, that of the Dinaric Alps is mostly karst. Karst is a soft limestone, easily eroded by wind and water. From an airplane some sections of the Interior Highlands look like raging white seas turned to stone. Beneath the petrified

Visitors can tour the Postojna Cave, partly by cable railway and partly on foot. The total length is fourteen miles (twenty-three kilometers).

seas flow real underground rivers—over a thousand of them. One, the Trebišnjica, is the longest underground river in the world. These rivers—and their ancestors—have shaped almost fifty thousand caves in the soft rock. The Postojna Cave in Slovenia is well known all over the world. German soldiers hid fuel in its vast chambers during World War II. But Yugoslav soldiers—and their time bombs—found the hiding place.

More than 90 percent of the karst caves in the Interior Highlands haven't been explored completely yet. That's great news for spelunkers. But so much karst is bad news for farmers in the region. Karst soil is thin and rocky. Here and there are *polje*, pockets in the karst where good soil has washed down and collected. Crops grow well in these *polje*. But there are not nearly enough of them to go around.

The countryside near the town of Plitvice in Croatia

Still, many people in the Interior Highlands are farmers. Yugoslav scientists are doing all they can to improve conditions for them. These scientists are working on the best ways to build reservoirs that will store some of the underground water where farmers can get at it. They have also built hydroelectric stations to harness some of the water's power.

Earthquakes are another problem for people who live in the highlands. Many quakes, of course, are small and cause little damage. But a huge one in 1963 destroyed most of the city of Skopje in Macedonia. Another big one, in 1979, did tremendous damage both in the southern Interior Highlands and in the Coastal Region of Montenegro.

A Yugoslav farm

A GREAT GREEN BLANKET

In the north-central part of Yugoslavia, the rocks finally stop— or at least disappear underground. This section is called the Pannonian Plains. It stretches like a great green blanket over much of Serbia and northern Croatia. Low hills curve up along the southern edge. But most of the land is flat and fertile, perfect for farming. And most of Yugoslavia's farming is done on the Pannonian Plains.

The plains are also the home of Yugoslavia's most important river, the Danube. Millions of years ago the Pannonian area was a huge lake. But over thousands and thousands of years, the Danube and its tributaries cut a giant gorge through the mountains at one end of the lake. The lake then drained out through the gorge, which is called the Iron Gates, and left the rich plains behind.

The fortress of Smederevo was built in the fifteenth century. During World War II it was damaged when explosives the Germans stored inside blew up.

In recent years the Danube at the Iron Gates has given another gift to Yugoslavia. From that point the river flows on into Rumania. Yugoslavia and Rumania have worked together to build a dam and hydroelectric project there. The dam provides a new source of power, a new lake, and better navigation on the river itself.

Workers near the dam site also uncovered a secret that had lain buried for an estimated eight thousand years. They found relics from an ancient human settlement, now called Lepenski Vir. Some archaeologists think it's the oldest human settlement discovered so far in Europe. Danube fishermen used crude stone tools to carve human faces found here. To protect the settlement from the waters of the Danube, it has been raised and a new museum has been built.

The Danube River isn't really as blue as Johann Strauss's waltz "The Beautiful Blue Danube" would lead one to believe. (Legend says it only seems to be that blue to people who are in love.) But to the Yugoslav people who live near it and enjoy its gifts, those muddy brown waters are certainly welcome, if not beautiful.

Skopje was badly damaged by an earthquake in 1963 and has been rebuilt.

OTHER GIFTS OF WATER

The Danube has also given four big tributaries to Yugoslavia: the Sava, the Drava, the Morava, and the Tisa. The Sava is the nation's longest river. It flows out of the Julian Alps in Slovenia and down through Croatia and Serbia. The Sava and Danube finally meet at the Serbian city of Belgrade. The Morava twists northward from southern Yugoslavia until it meets the Danube. All the Danube tributaries are important for farming, industry, and shipping.

Another important river is the Vardar. It flows south, through the middle of Macedonia's capital city, Skopje, and on into Greece and the Aegean Sea.

Lake Bled

Yugoslavia is also a land of many lakes. In Slovenia, Alpine lakes nestle in the snowcapped mountains. One of the most famous of these is Lake Bled, complete with castle, church, hot springs, ice-skating, and gorgeous scenery.

In Croatia lie the sixteen Plitvice Lakes. Each is a different color and each features cascades, falls, and lovely wooded shores. Some people think the Plitvice are the most beautiful lakes in the world. So many tourists have visited Plitvice National Park that the Yugoslav government has had to impose strict rules to keep the area from being destroyed by humans and their machines.

Fishing boats beached on the shores of the old town of Ohrid

Visitors now ride on a battery-operated train that doesn't pollute the air. Motorboats are forbidden on the waters.

Lake Scutari in Montenegro is Yugoslavia's largest lake. It has helped the people in this little republic with industry, tourism, hunting, and fishing. Many villagers have built their homes so close to the water's edge that they have to come and go by boat.

Ohrid is another important lake. It lies in Macedonia, on the Albanian border. In fact, only two thirds of Lake Ohrid is part of Yugoslavia. The rest belongs to Albania. Ohrid is the deepest lake in the Balkans. Its brilliant blue water has attracted more tourists than any other spot in Macedonia. They not only enjoy the lake and its abundance of fish, but they spend hours wandering through the charming old town of Ohrid on its shores.

Slano, a popular summer resort in the Coastal Region

A CHOICE OF CLIMATES

Yugoslavia offers almost any kind of climate, depending on geography and the seasons.

Along the Coastal Region some areas get as much annual sunshine as many other places in the world. This makes for mild, damp winters and hot, dry summers. Sometimes the temperature goes up to 100 degrees Fahrenheit (38 degrees Celsius) along the Adriatic. The Coastal Region also gets an especially high level of ultraviolet radiation. This means vacationers can get fantastic tans—or sunburns.

In general, short, cool summers and long, cold, snowy winters are usual for the Interior Highlands. On the Pannonian Plains the weather goes to surprising extremes. In summer, temperatures often hit 100 degrees Fahrenheit (38 degrees Celsius) and little rain falls. In winter, icy Arctic winds whip in from the northeast and temperatures dive into freezing ranges. Spring and fall bring heavy rains that often flood the Danube and its tributaries.

SOMETHING FOR EVERYONE

Yugoslavia's mixture of climates and geographical terrains has given her a mixture of plants and animals, too. Forests cover about 35 percent of the land and are an important natural resource. Oak, beech, chestnut, and evergreen trees grow in many mountainous areas. The dark evergreens that blanket the mountains are what gave Montenegro (Black Mountains) its name. Olive trees have grown in the Coastal Region since the days of the Greeks. Yugoslavia is working hard to plant more and more of these trees. Their fruit is used more for its oil than for eating.

Some unusual animals live in the forests, including black bears and lynx, both of which are rare today in Europe. Equally rare are the pelicans at Lake Scutari in Montenegro—along with thirty-four different kinds of fish.

Other waters in Yugoslavia are also filled with fish and other sea creatures. A small fishing boat in the Adriatic might catch an eel or a stingray or both in the same evening. In streams and lakes many kinds of freshwater fish can be caught. But the strangest water creature of all is the cave salamander found only in the underground streams of the Postojna Cave in Slovenia.

Unusual plants also thrive in various areas of Yugoslavia. Slovenia is full of Alpine blossoms, while Macedonia grows water lilies. One of Slovenia's most interesting plants is the *murka*. It has dark brown flowers that smell exactly like fine milk chocolate!

Yugoslavia has a rich variety of treasures underground, too. Iron, bauxite, chromite, coal, copper, lead, and zinc head the list. But there are many other minerals, so many that Yugoslavia is sometimes called "the mineralogical museum of Europe."

Because so much farming is done in Serbia, it is called Yugoslavia's breadbasket.

24

Chapter 3

A COMPLEX NATION

In Yugoslavia, each republic and province has its own special qualities. A closer look at each will help in understanding the country as a whole.

FORTRESSES, CHURCHES, AND BREAD

Serbia is the biggest, the flattest, and the strongest (at least it was in the past) of the republics. From one of Serbia's low hills, one can look in every direction and see nothing but field after field of growing cereal grain. Serbia is Yugoslavia's breadbasket.

Belgrade is the largest city in Yugoslavia and also the capital of both the Serbian republic and the entire nation.

Three things impress the visitor in Belgrade. First is the fact that everything—roads, buildings, everything—looks so modern. (That's because much of Belgrade had to be rebuilt after World War II.) Second is the different smell in the air—a good smell, but different from the smell back home. (It's probably a mixture of

Modern apartments in Belgrade

Sidewalk cafes in Belgrade are popular on sunny days.

cooking spices, Yugoslav tobacco, and the sort of coal some industries burn.) Third is the Cyrillic alphabet. Talk about different!

Belgrade looks over the point where the Danube and Sava rivers flow together. It's a beautiful spot and an important one strategically. Archaeologists say that people have lived in the area for seven thousand years. But there aren't many old buildings in Belgrade. Many invaders have fought over the city. Invasions began back before the time of the Romans and went on through the German occupation in World War II. All those battles left Belgrade a mass of ruins and ashes, but each time the city was rebuilt.

Today Belgrade is a modern city. Tall apartments and office buildings soar up to form a jagged skyline. The commercial center of the city is called Terazija. Here buildings loom and cars zoom. Fortunately, people on foot can cross many busy streets in Belgrade through "pedestrian subways" (tunnels under the street).

The old Parliament House, Belgrade

Sporting events take place at the new Sports Center beside the Danube. Both a supermarket and a department store are found in Belgrade House, the tallest building in the Balkans.

Across the Sava River lies "New Belgrade." It contains modern residential areas, a number of government buildings, and the Modern Art Museum. New Belgrade's construction after World War II was a challenge to architects because it is built mostly on marshland.

Massive Kalemegdan Fortress still watches over Belgrade's rivers. It's been destroyed and rebuilt again since the fourth century. Now it sits in a peaceful park where both Yugoslavs and tourists go to escape from the city's noise and busy activity.

Another favorite place to wander is Skadarska Street. This area has been rebuilt as it used to be, complete with cobblestone walks, cafés, musicians in folk costumes—and no cars. Serbs like to meet at the cafés. They sit drinking beer or wine, brandy or coffee, and eating spicy little sausages, along with Serbian bread.

The monastery at Sopocani, built in the thirteenth century, houses some beautiful medieval frescoes.

Old churches and religious art are easy to find in Serbia, from St. Mark's Church and many museums in Belgrade to grand old monasteries dotted across the countryside. One of the most beautiful monasteries is Kalenić, near the town of Rekovao. It was built in the early 1400s and looks as if a giant baker had frosted it in many colors.

There are log churches in Serbia, too. They were built during the Turkish occupation. Sometimes people used them for worship and sometimes as military outlooks. An old legend says that some Turks tried to burn one of these churches. But at once rain began to fall and put out the fire. The Turks never touched that church again. Most of the log churches still are used for worship today.

Smederevo Fortress, which stands alongside the Danube, was the last home of the Serbian rulers during the Middle Ages. When Smederevo fell to the Turks in 1459, the remnants of the Serbian state fell with it.

Serbia is a land of farmers who have been forced throughout their history to be soldiers. It's a land in which the Orthodox religion has been very important. Knocked down time after time by foreign invaders, it has gotten up each time to begin rebuilding for the future.

MORE BREAD AND FORTRESSES

Vojvodina, meaning "the duchy," is one of the two self-governing provinces. It is in northern Serbia. About half of the population are Serbs. But there are Hungarians, Croats, Slovaks, Rumanians, and fifteen other nationalities, too. That means many different languages are written and spoken there.

Vojvodina is also part of Yugoslavia's breadbasket. Only the hills of Vršac and Fruška Gora break her vast plain, which is crossed by six rivers. Vojvodina is the home of Lake Palić, a leftover from the huge ancient lake that drained out through the Iron Gates.

Novi Sad is Vojvodina's capital and biggest city. The name means "new garden." Soldiers first built here on the banks of the Danube across from a big old fortress called Petrovaradin. The residents of Novi Sad have fought as many floods throughout their history as they fought human invaders.

The planners of Novi Sad tried to keep the city in zones. Homes and apartments are in one section, industries in another, and recreational facilities in a third. Novi Sad is also known for its fine schools, art galleries, and museums.

The city of Sremska Mitrovica was built on the ruins of an old Roman city, called Sirmium. Sirmium was the birthplace of no fewer than five Roman emperors.

Vojvodina is also rich in fortresses, monasteries, churches, and colorful little villages.

INSIDE THE RING OF MOUNTAINS

South in Serbia, north of Macedonia, lies Kosovo-Metohija, often known simply as Kosovo. It is a little province, ringed by mountains and well watered by rivers and streams. Half of Kosovo is covered with forests and the rest with pastures and farmland. It's a poor land that the rest of Yugoslavia has been working hard to help. Mining is the most important industry, but factories are being built now, too.

Kosovo's population is mostly Albanian, but there are also Serbs, Montenegrins, Turks, and others. Although many new buildings have gone up in recent years, Kosovo still has a feel of the Orient about it. Both mosques and churches stretch toward the sky. Dishes such as mountain cheese and pickled peppers stuffed with beans still appear on menus.

Kosovo's capital city is Priština. In 1945 Priština didn't have a single paved street. Today there are many, plus new apartment and office buildings and a large university.

Not far from Priština lies the Kosovo Plain, site of a famous battle between the Serbs and the Turks in 1389. Serbia lost and her leader, Prince Lazar, died, but the Serbs killed Turkey's Sultan Murat I. Ever since, Serbs have celebrated the anniversary—June 28—as a national holiday. Visitors to the site can see the monument to the Serbian heroes and the sultan's tomb.

The Art Pavilion in Zagreb

A LITTLE BIT OF EVERYTHING

The republic of Croatia can offer visitors a little bit of everything. Part of Croatia is in the Pannonian Plains, part in the karst mountains, and part on the Adriatic Sea.

Most residents of Croatia are Croatians who speak Croatian. But Serbs, Slovenians, Hungarians, Italians, and Czechs live there, too, and preserve some of their own languages and customs.

Croatia's capital, Zagreb, is the second-largest city in Yugoslavia. It was founded by the Romans on twins hills not far from the Sava River. They called it Andauntonia. After the Romans came the Slavs, who changed the name to Zagreb. In later centuries, the Turks pounded again and again at her sturdy city walls. But they never got in. Zagreb still celebrates that fact by ringing her cathedral bell every day at 2:00 P.M.

For centuries, Zagreb has been known for excellent schools and museums and involvement in the arts. The Zagreb Soloists is one of the finest chamber music ensembles in the world. Makers of films

31

People enjoy strolling through a park (left) or window shopping on the busy streets (right) in Zagreb.

and cartoons in Zagreb have won many international awards. Zagreb is said to have an amazing total of 447 libraries.

For a taste of historic Zagreb, visit Gradec, which means "fortress." It's a fortified section that goes back to the Middle Ages. The roof of St. Mark the Evangelist Church is patterned in bright red, white, and blue tiles that form the emblems of Croatia and Zagreb. Modern artists have decorated part of the interior. The modern art blends well with those parts of the original sanctuary built in the fourteenth century. At noon each day a cannon is fired from Habernik Tower. That's been happening since the 1600s in Gradec. At night softly glowing gaslights illuminate the streets.

Not far from Zagreb are the Zagrebačka Gora Hills. In winter they're great for skiing. Visitors can sit back and eat stuffed turkey or suckling pig at one of the fine restaurants. In a nearby

The old market (left) and the palace of Diocletian (right) in Split.

museum is displayed the skeleton of the Krapina man. The discovery of this skeleton excited archaeologists because it's what is known as a "fossil man." Actually the remains of twenty-five to thirty prehistoric people were found at this site. So were the remains of animals, including a prehistoric hamster!

Split is a favorite stop in Croatia for history buffs. Here towers the palace of the Roman emperor Diocletian, a notorious persecutor of early Christians. Parts of the palace, including the emperor's tomb, have been almost perfectly preserved. Construction of the palace began in A.D. 295. It was used subsequently as a military camp, a market, and a shipping area. It covers about 30,000 square yards (25,084 square meters). Visitors can sit in the same courtyard Diocletian sat in or explore the maze of halls that runs beneath the palace. Split is not the only place with Roman ruins. The Croatian coast also has many.

Dubrovnik

Dubrovnik, on the southern part of Croatia's coast, is the most popular tourist spot in Yugoslavia. Officially it was ruled by a series of different regimes through the centuries, including Byzantium, the city-state of Venice, and Hungary. But in actual fact, it pretty much ruled itself, mostly by paying money to its enemies. The people of Dubrovnik were excellent shipbuilders and shrewd merchants.

There are many old buildings in Dubrovnik, which is closed to motor traffic. Most are found on the main street, Placa, including the lovely Sponza Palace, churches, squares, and fountains. Small streets worth investigating lead off Placa. One also can walk completely around the city on top of its medieval walls and see its white marble buildings.

34

Fields of lavender on Hvar (left), and Lovrijenac Fortress, Dubrovnik

No visit to Croatia is complete without a trip to her islands. One Yugoslav writer has called them stone ships in the Adriatic Sea. Each island offers its own surprise. There are fields of lavender on Hvar and mansions and churches on Korčula. There is a lace making school on Pag and a painting by Tintoretto on Korčula. Ruins and relics from almost any age can be found.

SKI SLOPES AND SNOW-WHITE HORSES

Snowy slopes and looking-glass lakes. Waterfalls and wild flowers. Castlelike caves and darting deer. That's Slovenia. Part of this republic is in the Julian Alps. But she does have some land on the Pannonian Plains and some on the Adriatic coast. The lovely Harbor of Roses (Portorož) is part of Slovenia, too.

The majority of people in Slovenia are Slovenes. They have their own language, Slovenian. But, like the other Yugoslav republics, Slovenia has her share of minority groups. Croats, Serbs, Hungarians, and Italians all speak their own languages.

SLOVENIA
Ljubljana
Belgrade

Ljubljana is a combination of old and new buildings.

Slovenia is another republic influenced by the West. This can be seen in the architecture of her old buildings and the many little Roman Catholic shrines along the roads. Most Slovenes are Roman Catholic.

Slovenia is the richest Yugoslav republic. There is a university in Ljubljana and many other institutions of higher learning. Just about everyone in Slovenia can read and write. She has produced many fine writers, artists, and musicians. She has also developed her industries, especially engineering, automobile manufacturing, and textiles.

Ljubljana is the capital of Slovenia. It's a bustling metropolis, but it's also a fairy-tale city. The Ljubljanica River runs through the city. A huge castle on a high hill in the middle of the city stands guard like a great stone lion. From the top of the castle, visitors can see a panorama of the city and its bridges with the

36

There is a riding school at Lipica, which was four hundred years old in 1980.

Julian Alps in the background. Fountains blossom everywhere like flowers. Churches are filled with art treasures.

Many buildings in Ljubljana were constructed during the baroque period of art. Baroque architects used an abundance of decorations and trimmings. The Franciscan Church is a good example of the baroque style.

Other towns across Slovenia are filled with beautiful buildings and art treasures, too. In winter, they're also havens for people who love snow sports. In summer, campers' tents pop up in the mountains like mushrooms. Not far from the town of Sežana is an unusual farm. The farm is called Lipica and on it are bred the world-famous white Lipizzaner horses. An Austrian archduke began the farm in 1580 so he would have pure-blooded white horses to pull the imperial coaches. Now the Lipizzaners are a special breed. They're elegant and graceful, high-stepping and smart, and well worth watching.

SEA OF STONE

Montenegro is the smallest republic. Sometimes she's called "the sea of stone." Hidden high in the stern karst mountains, her people have spent their history struggling with nature, invaders, and one another. The harshness of their life is reflected in their solemn red, black, and gold national costumes. It can be heard in the wild cries of their folk songs.

And yet, Montenegro is a beautiful land of rock, evergreens, and water. Giant Mount Durmitor (8,274 feet; 2,522 meters) wears a coat of forests dotted with glacial lakes. There are savage canyons, like those of the Piva and Tara rivers. Shepherds still roam the mountain pastures with their flocks. The silver leaves of two-thousand-year-old olive trees sparkle in the sun along the coast.

The people of Montenegro have not had much time for education until recent years. But there have always been a few who tried to improve the cultural life of their land. The dashing prince-bishop Njegoš was one of Montenegro's finest poets as well as one of her greatest leaders. He is buried on the summit of lovely Mount Lovćen. Inside the memorial is a statue of Njegoš with an eagle behind it. Another Montenegrin ruler brought a printing press to his homeland in 1493, just thirty-seven years after Gutenberg invented it. On it he had printed the first book ever done in the Cyrillic alphabet. It can be seen in the fifteenth-century Orthodox monastery in Cetinje.

Montenegro has her share of art treasures, including gold jewelry left by the Greeks and ruins left by the Romans. She has museums, monasteries, and churches, such as those in the city of Cetinje. The railings of the Vlaška Church in Cetinje were made from rifle barrels seized from the Turks. The monastery at Ostrog,

The restored houses in Sveti Stefan originally housed fishermen.

carved into the side of a mountain, looks like a huge white candle, shining down on the people below.

Montenegro has her share of vacation spots, especially on Lake Scutari and along the Adriatic coast. The village of Sveti Stefan originally was an island. After World War II it was practically deserted. The Montenegrins restored the red-tiled cottages into apartments for visitors. A causeway was built connecting it to the mainland. The refurbished cottages and fine beaches make Sveti Stefan a tourist haven.

The Bay of Kotor, seen from the highway snaking down the mountain to it, is one of the most beautiful sights in the world. Tiny towns cluster around the bay itself, eager to show off their treasures and their beaches.

Montenegro's capital city, Titograd, formerly Podgorica, lies on the banks of the Morača and Zeta rivers. It's an old city, in spite of its new name and modern buildings. Most pre-World War II buildings were destroyed in the earthquake of 1979. Much of its population is young, drawn from the surrounding mountains to find a better life.

Montenegro is a poor land. There simply isn't enough land to grow crops for her 600,000 people. Furthermore, she lost many of her leaders during World War II, when 76,000 Montenegrins were killed. The other Yugoslav republics are working with her in every way they can. When an earthquake leveled the old town of Budva in 1979, help poured in from both Yugoslavia and abroad.

STONES AND SPICES

Bosnia-Hercegovina is the third-largest Yugoslav republic, both in size and in population. Although she does have a tiny coastline, most of Bosnia-Hercegovina lies in the mountains. She's had a troubled history, full of invasions. For four hundred years she lived under the Turks. Then Austria-Hungary took over. Now in her cities, Muslim mosques and minarets rub shoulders with Catholic and Orthodox churches and modern office buildings. Bosnia is truly a mixture of East and West.

Her people are a mixture, too. Thirty-two percent are Serbs, 40 percent Muslims, 18 percent Croats, and the rest other ethnic groups. About 50 percent of the people farm, and mining is also an important industry.

The capital of Bosnia-Hercegovina is Sarajevo. Its name comes from a Turkish word that means "square before the palace." That

The Husref Bey Mosque was built for the Turkish governor, Gazi Husref Bey, in the sixteenth century.

dates back to the 1400s when the Turkish governor's palace was the center of the town. Today Sarajevo stands as a symbol in concrete and stone of the mixture of peoples and cultures in Bosnia's history. Following the Turkish influence, the old Muslim houses in the city's center are built with gardens in the back. They cluster around the mosque and are reached through small winding alleys. Inside, the houses are furnished with low benches, big pillows, and Turkish carpets.

Almost everyone in Sarajevo visits the bazaar every day. Here coppersmiths and goldsmiths, quiltmakers and leather workers ply their trades where everyone can watch. Many of the streets are named for the craftsmen who worked—and still work—there. Woolen rugs, Turkish pipes, and pieces of embroidery can be purchased. The shopkeepers will contend that people simply can't live without their merchandise. And they'll be very disappointed if the customers don't bargain over the prices. The bazaar is filled with smells of onions and spices, roasting meat and Turkish coffee.

Away from Sarajevo are Bosnia's glorious mountains. One section is even called "Little Switzerland." Here sports enthusiasts

41

*On July 27 each year, a diving competition is held
on the old bridge over the Neretva River in Mostar.*

can hike and hunt, and, in winter, ski. There are rare types of wild
flowers and rivers filled with trout.

The old city of Mostar is built of stone on the Neretva River.
There are many Oriental-style buildings and a long, graceful,
curved bridge over the Neretva built in 1556. During the summer,
boys from Mostar make spectacular dives from this bridge as
crowds watch and applaud.

Mosques and minarets dot the skyline. One particularly beautiful mosque is the sixteenth-century Karadžoz Beg with its attractive exterior and wonderful decorations inside.

TRAGEDY AND COURAGE

Macedonia's weather is unusual—cold and wet in winter and subtropical in summer. Once again, climate is affected by geography. Macedonia is a series of high mountains and low fertile valleys. Her closeness to the Aegean Sea gives her mild weather, especially in the Vardar River valley.

Most of Macedonia's people are Macedonians who speak Macedonian. The majority belong to the Orthodox church, though a minority are Muslims. But many Turks and Albanians live in Macedonia, too. They make up the Muslim minority, though some of the Albanians are Roman Catholic.

The history of Macedonia itself goes back almost three thousand years. Alexander the Great (356-323 B.C.) came from there when Macedonia controlled ancient Greece. The Apostle Paul had a vision that he should preach there. But the history of the present republic has nothing to do with that ancient Macedonia. The Slavs, the ancestors of the present Macedonians, arrived at the end of the 400s and the beginning of the 500s.

Skopje, the capital of Macedonia

It was a bloody, war-torn future that awaited them. Disaster after disaster and invader after invader shook Macedonia. Her people had to struggle hard to survive. Although they spoke Macedonian, they had no alphabet and no books to teach their children to read and write the language. Many stories were passed on from generation to generation in folk songs. Today, as part of Yugoslavia, Macedonia has established her alphabet and literary language, along with many schools and technical institutes.

She also has a brand-new capital. In 1963, a tremendous earthquake destroyed the old city of Skopje. It wasn't the first time the city had been leveled. Other earthquakes did it in the sixth and the sixteenth centuries. Skopje is used to picking up and starting over. With help from all over the world, she did it again in 1963. But her tragic history explains why her oldest church, St. Savior, goes back only about two hundred years. That's young for a Yugoslav church.

Old buildings can be found near Bitola, the second-largest town

44

The center of Bitola

in Macedonia. Here is the site of an ancient Greek-Roman city called Heraclea Lyncestis. Only about 5 percent of the site has been excavated so far.

In the countryside of Macedonia are fruit trees and vineyards and tobacco fields. Almost all the farmers raise tobacco; they dry it in courtyards, on housefronts, and even in the attics of their homes.

The town of Ohrid is near the Albanian border. It's an ancient town, huddled on the shores of Lake Ohrid under the protecting walls of a fortress that goes back at least twenty-five hundred years. There's religious art and architecture in Ohrid and a music festival. The modern section of Ohrid has mosques and houses of Turkish architecture. It is a popular resort area. Lake Ohrid has many kinds of fish. The belvica is found nowhere else in Europe.

So, troubled though her history has been, Macedonia has treasures to share. Folk traditions have remained unchanged and visitors can find wonderful handmade articles, such as rugs and wood carvings.

Because the acoustics of the Roman amphitheater in Pula are so excellent, it is used for an annual international song competition, an annual film festival, and opera performances.

Chapter 4

INVASIONS
AND CONQUERORS

LAND AT THE CROSSROADS

The land now called Yugoslavia has had a long and complicated history. It sits at the crossroads of two worlds, the East and the West. For centuries, invaders have been trampling into Yugoslavia from both worlds, fighting for the right to live there and control its land and people.

The first inhabitants of Yugoslavia were there over 100,000 years ago, according to archaeologists. But little is known about them. The first settlers that ancient historians wrote about were the Illyrians and Thracians, who lived about three thousand years ago. Then, during the seventh century B.C., the Greeks moved in. They set up trading communities along the coast of the Adriatic Sea, as well as inland settlements. During the sixth century B.C., Celtic tribes arrived, but the Greeks stayed on. Some of their beautiful pillars and statues are still in existence.

By A.D. 1, the Romans had conquered the whole area. They made it into a Roman province and called it Illyricum. Then, in about A.D. 350, the Roman Empire split into two parts. That division ran down the middle of what is now Yugoslavia and has affected her history ever since. The western part was controlled by Rome. It included the areas that eventually became Croatia, Slovenia, and some of Bosnia. The eastern part was controlled by Constantinople (now called Istanbul). It included Serbia, Montenegro, and Macedonia.

Once the Roman invaders had settled into their new province, they were kept busy fighting off tribes of barbarians. Goths, Huns, Ostrogoths, Gepids, Sarmatians, Bulgars, and Avars all swarmed down on them. Some of the barbarians' foot soldiers were Slavic people from southern Poland and Russia. During the sixth century A.D., these Slavic soldiers and their families came to the new land to stay. Here they became known as "southern Slavs."

For hundreds of years these Slavs lived together in family groups or agricultural communes called *zadrugas*. The oldest man (or sometimes the oldest woman) was head of a group. Everyone worked together to grow crops, raise animals, and protect the group from outsiders. In some parts of Yugoslavia, people continued living in zadrugas until the middle of the twentieth century.

Some zadrugas, of course, produced more powerful leaders than others. Little by little, certain family groups took charge of other family groups. Eventually separate kingdoms developed, such as Serbia and Slovenia. The people in the east and south became Eastern Orthodox Christians and wrote in the Cyrillic alphabet. Those in the north and west became Roman Catholic Christians and used the Roman alphabet. One group of people in Bosnia formed their own brand of Christianity during a period of religious persecution in the Middle Ages. They were called Bogomils. The Bogomils no longer exist, but they left some large,

SOME ARTIFACTS FOUND IN BOSNIA

2 and 3. Cursive script on a manuscript and a stone monument from the eighteenth century
4. A stone seat from the fifteenth century
5. A headdress woven of dried flax and stalks occasionally worn by the women.
6 and 7. Two sides of a bronze coin from the fourteenth century
8. A gravestone showing a stag hunt from about 1400.
9. A gravestone showing a family of three men, five women, and two children being led
in a dance by a leader, from around 1400.

Bogomil tombstones

strange, carved tombstones that still stand in the Bosnian
mountains.

As the various kingdoms grew and became stronger, their
histories began to take different directions. To get an idea of what
happened overall, it's best to look first at what happened in each
kingdom.

SERBIA

Serbia was the strongest of the kingdoms. At first it was
controlled by the Byzantine (Eastern) Empire. The state of
Bulgaria fought many wars with the Byzantine Empire over
Serbia, but always lost. By 1168, though, both Bulgaria and the

Byzantine Empire had grown weak. This gave some Serbian brothers of the Nemanjić family the opportunity to take power. They ruled well and soon Serbia was bigger and richer than ever. The last great Nemanjić king, Stephan Dušan, in 1331 made himself emperor and even planned to conquer the Byzantine Empire. He died before he got the chance to try, but he is still an important hero in Serbia.

Then, during the 1300s, an extremely powerful enemy—the Turks from Asia—began invading Serbia again and again. Serbia finally fell to the Turks at the tragic battle of Kosovo in 1389. Her leader, Prince Lazar, was killed. Those nobles who survived the battle had to flee to other countries. Many popular ballads were written about that sad day at Kosovo. Serbian people still haven't forgotten it.

They also haven't forgotten the dark days under Turkish rule. The Turks were Muslims; any Serb who refused to become a Muslim was treated much like a slave. Serbs had to pay taxes to the Turks and do forced labor. Each year the Turks took a large group of Serbian boys to Turkey, raised them as Muslims, and trained them to be soldiers for the Turkish sultan. Serbs were forbidden to ride horses when Turks were nearby, wear fine clothes, or own arms. Punishment for offenders was so cruel that some Serbs fled to the mountains and became bandits. Called *hajduks*, they did all they could to harass the Turks. Many ballads were sung about them, too.

But in spite of all these hardships, most Serbs refused to give up their Orthodox religion. In their minds and hearts, it helped identify them as a separate, individual country. Serbian priests even led revolts against the Turks. These always failed, but they helped keep alive the spirit of the people.

Karadjordje

Prince Miloš Obrenović

At last, during the late 1600s and the 1700s, Turkey began to grow weak. France was at war with her, as were Austria and Russia. In 1804 the Serbs decided to revolt. Their leader was a pig-trader known as Karadjordje. His name means "Black George." Russia helped Serbia with men and money for the uprising, but Serbia didn't have to ask anyone for courage. By 1808 Serbia had won partial freedom.

In 1813 the Turks conquered Serbia again, but only two years later another leader, Miloš Obrenović, led a successful second revolt. By 1829 Serbia was declared autonomous (self-governing, but still under Turkish overlordship). Prince Miloš was an absolute ruler and the wealthiest man in Serbia. He divided the confiscated Turkish property among the peasants, who made up most of the Serbian people.

Petar I, king of Yugoslavia from 1919 to 1921 and king of Serbia from 1903 to 1918

Little Serbia gradually developed and grew stronger, sometimes with Russia's help. In 1830 hardly anyone, including Prince Miloš, could read and write. Then schools were built and their graduates went to universities in Europe. An able statesman, Ilija Garašanin, organized the police force and government. His "Outline" (*Načertanije*) of 1844 set the goal of uniting all Serbs, then all southern Slavs, around Serbia. After two wars with Turkey, Serbia won full independence in 1878.

Then in 1903 the last Obrenović ruler was overthrown. Under King Petar I, Serbia became a constitutional kingdom with complete political freedom and civil rights. Austria plotted ways to crush her, and in 1878 occupied neighboring Bosnia and Hercegovina. In 1914 a Serbian secret society, composed mostly of nationalist army officers and called "Unity or Death," helped a Bosnian patriot, Gavrilo Princip, assassinate Austria's Archduke Francis Ferdinand in Sarajevo. That murder set off events that led to the deaths of thousands. Austria-Hungary invaded Serbia, touching off World War I.

The rocky slopes of the mountains in southern Yugoslavia are poor farmland and suitable only for raising livestock.

MONTENEGRO

The tiny mountain kingdom of Montenegro perches high above her neighbors. In the early days her rocky slopes helped protect her from many of the problems and invaders that beset the lower Yugoslav kingdoms.

Montenegro has always been a poor land. The rocky slopes and a few pastures are usable only for raising cattle, sheep, and bees. That's what kept the old people, women, and children busy.

Montenegro's men, though, kept busy in another way— fighting. They helped their Serbian and Croatian neighbors battle the Turks. Unfortunately, they were just as good at fighting one another.

Montenegrins lived in large family groups, or clans. If a member of one clan insulted, hurt, or killed a member of another clan, the men of the second clan felt they had to take their revenge in blood. Feuds between clans sometimes went on for generations. Contemporary Montenegrin writer Milovan Djilas says his great-grandfather, two grandfathers, father, uncle, and brothers all died in feuds.

For a few hundred years, Montenegro technically was ruled by Turkey. But the Turks rarely were able to get up into the mountains to enforce their rule. So the Montenegrin families kept most of their power. Montenegro had chosen the Orthodox faith. For many years her head bishop was also her military leader. Most famous of these prince-bishops was a man known simply as Njegoš. He ruled from 1830 to 1851 and tried to educate his people and modernize his country. Njegoš was also a fine poet.

Finally, in the late 1800s, Montenegro won territory from the Turks and soon became independent. Her good friend Russia sent money to buy guns and win still more land, including some territory on the coast of the Adriatic Sea. But all the fighting left her weak and, in spite of more lands, poor.

MACEDONIA

Macedonia once extended south to the Aegean Sea in what is now part of Greece. It is a perfect land for trade routes, and trade routes mean riches. But they also mean wars and invaders who want those riches. In early days, first Greeks, then Romans, then Byzantines moved into Macedonia. The Slavs came during the sixth century. At the end of the ninth century, Bulgaria took over. But less than a hundred years later, Macedonia had its own

The remains of a Turkish tower (left) and a Macedonian icon from the fourteenth century

emperor, Samuel, who also ruled Bulgaria. After he died, the Byzantines took control again until Serbia won most of the territory during the 1300s.

Until then, most of the Macedonian Slavs had been Orthodox Christians. But after the Serbs, the Turks thundered down on Macedonia and stayed for over five hundred years. During the Turkish reign, some Macedonians became Muslims.

In 1912, Greek, Bulgar, and Serb armies warred against the Turks and drove them out. Then the victorious allies argued over dividing up Macedonia and fought another war among themselves. Eventually Macedonia found herself chopped up among Serbia, Bulgaria, and Greece.

Meanwhile, Macedonia simply wanted to be left alone, free and in peace. Sometimes revolutionaries tried to win those goals for her. Two of the most famous were Damian Gruev and Goce Delčev. They fought in the late 1800s and are remembered as heroes in Macedonia today. But freedom, peace, and prosperity still lay far ahead in Macedonia's future.

BOSNIA-HERCEGOVINA

Bosnia-Hercegovina was another land that seemed doomed never to have peace, freedom, and prosperity. Croatia was her neighbor on two sides and Serbia on the other two. Both wanted Bosnia-Hercegovina for themselves. Their separate churches wanted the land, too. Croatia would have forced the Bosnians to become Roman Catholic. Serbia would have pushed the Orthodox church. All this fighting was one reason so many Bosnians founded their own Bogomil religion.

For about 150 years, Bosnia-Hercegovina managed to exist as a free kingdom. Her most famous ruler was Kulin, who ruled from 1180 to 1203. But even during this period, life was difficult for most people. A few noble families continually fought with one another and tried to control the lower classes. Then there were the invaders from Serbia, Croatia, and Hungary.

The Turks started invading at the end of the 1300s. Many of the Bosnians became Muslims. But the Turks turned out to be cruel visitors. Finally, during the 1800s, the peasants in Bosnia-Hercegovina began revolting. They hoped for help from the rest of the European world.

Many Europeans took the side of the Bosnians. But politics turned out to be stronger than sympathy. Bosnia-Hercegovina revolted against Turkish rule in 1875, but in 1878 the European powers handed over the little land to Austria. The Austrians built roads and railways and set up some industries. But they did nothing to help the farmers who were all but slaves to the landlords. And most people in Bosnia-Hercegovina were farmers.

At the end of World War I, in 1918, Bosnia-Hercegovina became part of Yugoslavia.

Busy Zagreb, the capital of Croatia (above)
Dubrovnik, a port on the Adriatic Sea (below)

A narrow street in Dubrovnik (left) and a bronze statue of Bishop Gregory of Nin, which was sculpted by a native Croatian, Ivan Meštrović

CROATIA

For many years the area now called Croatia was made up of three kingdoms—Croatia, Slavonia, and Dalmatia. But most of the people in all three were Croatians. In fact, the three kingdoms were often known as the Triune Kingdom.

Croatia lies in the northern and western parts of Yugoslavia. That means she has always had more ties with Europe than with the East. Many of her old buildings resemble those in Austria or Italy and most of her people have been Roman Catholic.

Croatia also has had problems with invaders. Up until the 1300s, the Byzantines claimed to be in charge. But other people, such as the Franks, the Bulgarians, the Normans from Sicily, the Tartars, and the Magyars from Hungary, tried their luck. The

Venetians (from the Italian city-state of Venice) ruled most of Dalmatia from the 1200s to the 1700s. All in all, Croatia was a free and independent kingdom only from 910 till 1102.

In 1102 her last king died. He did not have any children. So Croatia asked the Hungarian king to become her ruler. From then on, Croatia and Hungary had a special relationship, sometimes bad, sometimes good. But the Croats never forgot their own heritage and ways of doing things.

This led to serious internal problems. As in Bosnia-Hercegovina, most of the land in Croatia was owned by a few noble families. The peasants had to work on the land under conditions of poverty. From 1526 till 1699, the Turks occupied most of Croatia and Hungary. But that didn't change conditions for the peasants. They were still miserable and, finally, began to rebel.

One of the biggest rebellions occurred in 1573. It was led by a man called Matija Gubec. The rebellion failed and Gubec was executed. But the peasants went on trying—again and again.

Eventually the Austrians (who had built up an empire with the Hungarians) ruled in Croatia. Because of revolutions in their own empire, they had to free the Croatian peasants and divide the land among them. But most peasants got just a scrap of land, so they were still very poor.

Then during the 1800s, a new idea was born in Croatia. The people didn't want to be ruled by anyone else. They wanted to be a free country. A political party was formed to work toward this goal. Croatia even helped Austria fight some Hungarian rebels so Austria would then assist in the Croatian battle for independence. But Austria decided not to offer help. Soon Hungary was in charge of large parts of Croatia again.

A building used for storing hay

The peasants paid little attention to all of these political games. They were too busy trying to stay alive. Conditions in the towns improved a little at the beginning of the twentieth century. But life on the farms was still harsh and bleak. Finally, in 1905, two brothers decided to form a political party to help the peasants. Antun and Stefan Radić called their party the Croat Peasant party. It would turn out to be a very important force in Croatia's future.

SLOVENIA

Slovenia's history has been a little different from that of the other Yugoslav republics. The Turks never managed to stay in Slovenia when they were invading her neighbors. Although other countries did rule her—Slovenia was never free—they weren't as fierce and destructive as the Turks.

The architecture of Piran in Slovenia shows the Italian influence.

Slavic people first came to Slovenia during the sixth century. In almost no time, German rulers took over the government. In the 1500s, the Austrian Empire took charge and the Slovene people remained part of that empire until 1918, when Yugoslavia was born.

The Slovenes became Roman Catholics and used the Roman alphabet. But they held on to their own language—Slovene—throughout the centuries, even though they weren't allowed to use it officially or teach it in schools until after 1848. Slovene children grew up speaking two languages—Slovene and German.

The national costume of Slovenia

The Slovenes also held on to their own traditions in arts, crafts, clothing, literature, and music. Life in rural areas was very hard for many centuries because Slovenia is not a good place for farming. But at least the land wasn't torn apart by one invader after another.

During the 1800s, conditions improved for the farmers. Many of them became educated and could take advantage of new farming methods. Many also began working together in agricultural cooperatives. As industries grew, some farmers left for jobs in factories or mines. This meant there was more land for the farmers who remained.

The Slovenes were proud of their progress. They were also proud of the fact that they were southern Slavs. So, when their southern Slav neighbors began talking about forming a nation of their own, the Slovenes were more than ready to join them.

A monument to war dead at Rovinj

Chapter 5

PUTTING THE REPUBLICS TOGETHER

THE FIRST MOVE

Gavrilo Princip started it all. On June 28, 1914, he assassinated Austria's Archduke Francis Ferdinand in the Bosnian city of Sarajevo. At that time the Austro-Hungarian Empire controlled Slovenia, Croatia, and Bosnia-Hercegovina. Its rulers believed Serbia had planned the assassination. (Actually, one of her secret societies *had* helped Princip.) So Austria-Hungary declared war on Serbia and World War I began.

It was a hard war for Serbia. She had far fewer soldiers and military supplies than Austria-Hungary. But she held on bravely for over a year, in spite of a typhus epidemic that killed more of her men than the enemy did.

By December of 1915, facing Austrian, German, and Bulgarian armies, the Serbian army had to retreat. But it would not surrender. Instead it fled to Montenegro and Albania to wait for help from the Allies (those nations fighting Germany and the

65

A painting of the assassination of Archduke Francis Ferdinand in 1914 by an eyewitness, Felix Schwormstadt (left) and the Archduke's assassin, Gavrilo Princip

other Central Powers). Thousands of soldiers died in the harsh winter weather. Those who survived were finally evacuated by the Allies to the island of Corfu. Later they served with the Allies on the Salonika front and led the attack that drove the enemy out of Serbia at last.

In 1918 the war ended. Germany and Austria-Hungary were defeated and the southern Slav people were finally free to form their own country. It was a moment for which they had waited a long time.

Alexander was regent from 1918 to 1921. He became king in 1921 and ruled until he was assassinated in 1934.

A HARD BIRTH

December 1, 1918, was the big day, the birthday of the Kingdom of the Serbs, Croats, and Slovenes. Actually the new nation included Serbia, Croatia, Slovenia, Bosnia-Hercegovina, Montenegro, and some of Macedonia. King Petar I of Serbia was proclaimed king of the whole nation. But Petar was ill, so his son, Alexander, ruled for him. In 1921 Petar died and Alexander became king in his own right.

Uniting all those separate lands into one country was an immense job. The southern Slavs found themselves with numerous problems. The Slovenes and the Croatians thought the Serbs had too much power. The Serbs thought they deserved all the power they had.

Then, in 1929, King Alexander set aside the constitution and began to rule as a dictator. Alexander decreed that the new country was to be called Yugoslavia, with no political parties and a censored press. He announced he would divide the country into sections that he alone would designate.

Alexander's decrees did not go over well with many of the people. In 1934 some Croatian terrorists murdered him. His son, Petar II, was only eleven at the time, so Alexander's cousin, Prince Paul, took over the government. But Paul's policies weren't much different from Alexander's.

DARK YEARS OF GLORY

In 1939 World War II began. It shook Yugoslavia just as it shook every other nation in Europe. Originally the war was between the Allies (led by Great Britain and France) and the Axis powers (led by Germany and Italy). Yugoslavia wasn't strong enough to fight in such a war. The hope was to remain friends with both sides while devoting most of the young nation's energy to self-development.

But the German government began to put on pressure. On March 25, 1941, the Yugoslav government decided to side with the Axis. Serbian generals, who disagreed with this decision, promptly overthrew Paul's government and gave the throne to Petar, who was now seventeen.

On April 6 the Germans invaded Yugoslavia. The infant Yugoslav army disintegrated in the face of the powerful German war machine and surrendered after eleven days. Petar and other governmental leaders escaped to England.

But the Yugoslav people hadn't finished fighting. In fact, they

King Petar II with United States President Franklin Delano Roosevelt in 1942

had only begun. The Germans promptly divided up their country. Part went to Italy, part to Bulgaria, and part Germany kept for herself. Much of Croatia and Bosnia-Hercegovina was handed over to the terrorist group that had murdered King Alexander. Some Yugoslavs decided to cooperate with the Germans. But many, many others banded together to fight the enemy — in any and every way they could.

The people who resisted the Germans belonged to two groups. The Chetniks were led by Draža Mihailović, a Serbian army officer. The Chetniks supported King Petar's government. A

69

Josip Broz Tito

young Communist from Croatia, Josip Broz Tito, led the other group, the Partisans. He wanted Yugoslavia to have a Communist government. Soon these two groups began to fight one another. At first the Allies tried to help the Chetniks. But soon they discovered that the Partisans seemed to be fighting harder against the Germans. So they began sending supplies and weapons to Tito's forces.

The Partisans fought one bloody battle after another to free different areas of their country. Men and women fought side by side. Even very old people and children did all they could to help. They blew up German trains or bridges. They smuggled supplies to the Partisans. They cared for wounded soldiers.

The Freedom Monument in Kruševo

A young girl named Marjanca Žurga was out walking one day when she found an English pilot trapped in a tree. His plane had been shot down by the Germans and he had parachuted out. The pilot was wounded and couldn't walk. The Germans were searching the area for him.

Marjanca could have let the Germans find the pilot. That would have been the safe thing to do. But Marjanca cared more for her country than she did for her safety. She ran for her mother and they carried the pilot to their house. There they fed him and cared for his wounds. Then they sent a message to Marjanca's father, who was a Partisan. He and his men managed to get the pilot to a Partisan base where he would be protected.

German troops capture a group of Partisans in the mountains of Croatia. This photograph was taken in 1943.

There are thousands of stories like Marjanca's. The resistance groups in World War II took some terrible risks. The Germans tortured and killed anyone they caught helping the Partisans, the Chetniks, or the Allies. Sometimes they even killed thousands of old people, women, and children in a city just because the Partisans were fighting in the surrounding area. But they could not kill the people's spirit or put a halt to their resistance.

In 1944, the Partisans, with some help from the Russian army, drove the Germans out of Belgrade and the rest of Yugoslavia. At once Tito set up a Communist government. The Germans and their sympathizers fled.

Tito was in power, but he didn't want the rest of the world to think he had stolen that power from his people. So, in November of 1945, he held an election. All citizens over the age of eighteen could vote. All enlisted men and women could vote no matter what their age. Other political parties were not permitted to campaign and their leaders were arrested. When the votes were counted, Tito's Communists, by intimidation and pressure, had won an overwhelming victory. The Partisans had prevailed in the civil war with the Chetniks and controlled Yugoslavia.

TITO'S WAY

The first thing Tito did was to eliminate all other political parties. Draža Mihailović, the patriotic Chetnik leader, was given a sham trial and executed. All opposition was crushed ruthlessly. The Communists assumed total control in Yugoslavia. The head of the Roman Catholic church in Yugoslavia, Archbishop Stepinac of Zagreb, was arrested, tried, and sentenced to sixteen years hard labor.

On November 29, 1945, Tito's rubber-stamp parliament met. It announced that Yugoslavia would no longer be ruled by kings. From now on she would be known as the Federal People's Republic of Yugoslavia. She would be made up of six republics: Serbia, Croatia, Slovenia, Bosnia-Hercegovina, Montenegro, and Macedonia. Serbia would also include two autonomous provinces: Vojvodina and Kosovo-Metohija. Each republic and province would have a voice in how it was governed.

Tito also had to find a way to feed, clothe, and house the many people whose lives had been shattered by the war. He had to set up a system of money that would work. He had to divide the land fairly and put industry back on its feet.

The world soon saw that Tito's way was communism. The constitution passed in January of 1946 was a virtual copy of that of the Soviet Union. But Tito was not about to take orders from that nation. This angered Joseph Stalin, ruler in the Soviet Union. In 1948 he broke off relations between his country and Yugoslavia. The Cominform, an organization of mostly east European Communist parties controlled by the Soviet Union, threw Yugoslavia out of the Soviet bloc and blockaded her. Yugoslavia still desperately needed help to recover from the devastation of the war. So she turned to Western nations, including the United States. They were more than happy to keep her free of Soviet Union influence and supplied her with food and weapons.

As the years passed, Tito made it clear that although his way was communism, it would be his own brand of communism. The republics and provinces gained a good bit of control over their local governments. Workers had a say in how their industries were run. The constitution was revised several times, with all changes initiated and approved by Tito.

Today only one political party is permitted in Yugoslavia—the Communist party (officially the League of Communists of Yugoslavia). Party members play active roles in government.

The republics and provinces are divided into 508 communes. Voters in each commune choose members of a local assembly and a communal council. These local government officials vote for those who serve on an assembly for the republic or province. The people on the republican assembly choose an executive council for their area.

Laws for the whole country are made by the Federal Assembly. It is divided into two houses. One house is called the Federal

Chamber and the other the Chamber of the Republics and Autonomous Provinces. The whole Federal Assembly chooses members of the cabinet, which is called the Federal Executive Council. Cabinet members are heads of government departments. Their president is Yugoslavia's premier.

But the highest government body in Yugoslavia is the presidency. It consists of nine members, one from each republic and province, plus the premier. All decisions must be unanimous. Yugoslavia knew it would be difficult to find another leader like Tito. So, under his guidance, she set up the presidency in 1974. Since then it has determined most of her policies. The people serving on it were ready to take over when Tito died in 1980.

Yugoslavia has four kinds of courts. There are civil courts, criminal courts, and military courts on three levels—federal, republic, and local. Then there are "self-management" courts that deal with problems between businesses.

Is Tito's way still working in Yugoslavia? Today, like other east European countries, she faces a grave economic crisis. She is politically unstable, too. There have been serious political problems as Albanian Muslims in Kosovo seek either to become a separate republic or to join Albania. Milovan Djilas, a high government official who criticized Communist programs, has spent much time in prison or under house arrest. Some Croatian groups want Croatia to be an independent country. Nevertheless, many people consider Yugoslavia to be a basically healthy country with good future prospects.

Since Tito's death, she has shown how well he planned for her to continue without him. But most important, she has proved to the world that she can be a strong, united nation of the southern Slavs.

Winter in the mountains of southern Yugoslavia

Chapter 6

SPECIAL SONS
AND DAUGHTERS

In the history of every nation, certain people stand out and seem bigger than life. They have special gifts that help shape the destiny of their country. Yugoslavia has had many such sons and daughters. Here are only a few of them.

PRINCE OF THE MOUNTAINS

Petar Petrović Njegoš was born in Montenegro in 1813. As a prince and a bishop, he was known by his nickname, Rade. As a poet, he was known simply as Njegoš.

Njegoš came from a poor but proud clan, a clan of leaders. For a while Njegoš studied with a priest at Topla and for a while longer at the Cetinje monastery. Mostly, though, he taught himself. His Uncle Petar, a bishop and ruler of Montenegro, was his great hero.

Njegoš grew up to be tall and handsome. When he was only seventeen, his uncle died and the family decided Njegoš should succeed him. One day Njegoš was a student; the next day he was a monk, a bishop, and a ruler of Montenegro. Njegoš met the challenge bravely. During his life he strengthened Montenegro's government, organized the courts and economy, built the first primary school, and set up a printing house. Meanwhile, he also fought the Turks and wrote poetry that sang the story of his land. Two lines from his most famous poem, *The Mountain Wreath*, say a lot about Njegoš and about Montenegro:

> The thorny crown is sharp, sweet after be the fruit!
> Except by the way of death was never resurrection.

Njegoš wrote a poem, *The Ray of the Microcosm*, based on *Paradise Lost* by John Milton. It is considered Yugoslavia's most important philosophical poem. Njegoš died in 1851 after a long illness. As he had requested, he was buried on his beloved Mount Lovćen.

LOVER OF STONE

A memorial to Njegoš was designed by another of Yugoslavia's special sons, Ivan Meštrović. Meštrović was born in 1883. He grew up in a poor, mountainous area of Croatia. His father was the only person in the village who could read and write.

Even as a child, Meštrović loved to work with stone. When he was fifteen, some people in his village helped his father send him to the city of Split to study with a stonecutter. From there he went on to Vienna to study. It wasn't long before he was known all over the world as a great sculptor.

In 1941, during World War II, Meštrović was put under house arrest by Germany's puppet government in Croatia. Released in

A bronze sculpture of an Indian by Meštrović is in Chicago, Illinois.

1942, he traveled to Rome. In 1954 he became a citizen of the United States. Meštrović died in 1962.

His sculptures are huge, solid pieces. They seem to grow naturally from the rocky strength of his native land and his religious faith. Many are of religious or patriotic subjects. Some of the most famous include *My Mother at Prayer, Pieta, Job,* the Tomb of the Unknown Soldier on Avala outside Belgrade, and the memorial to Njegoš.

BOSNIA'S STORYTELLER

Bosnia also has produced her share of patriots. One of these is Ivo Andrić, who was born in the town of Travnik in 1892. His father died when Andrić was only two. His mother then took the family to live with relatives. Andrić had to support himself during much of the time he spent obtaining an education. But he went all the way to receive the Ph.D. degree.

After this he joined the diplomatic service and began writing stories. He was Yugoslav ambassador in Berlin when Germany invaded Yugoslavia. After World War II Andrić turned to writing novels. Two of these—*Bosnian Story* and *The Bridge on the Drina*—are among his most famous works.

Andrić's writing shows his fierce love for Bosnia, her history, and her people. But he also feels his stories hold truths for every person in every place. "Everyone has his country in which he takes the test of life," he once said.

In 1961 Ivo Andrić received the Nobel Prize in literature, the highest international award any writer can receive.

HARVESTER OF SONGS

A young man named Stefan Mokranjac chose music as his way of serving his Serbian homeland. Mokranjac was born in 1856 in the town of Negotin. He studied in Belgrade, Munich, Rome, and Leipzig. Then he became conductor of the Belgrade Choral Society, which he led in tours all over Europe.

Meanwhile, Mokranjac was also composing, mostly choral music. He originated a type of song for chorus that he called a *rukovet.* The word means "a handful of harvested goods." What Mokranjac harvested were the folk songs of his people. These he set in beautiful choral pieces that carried the voice of Serbia around the world.

Mokranjac's ideas and music influenced many later composers. He died in 1914 after a long illness. But his music is still sung and he is still remembered as one of the great composers of Yugoslav music.

The Croatian National Theater in Zagreb (above)
The International Folk Festival (below left) is held annually in Zagreb.
A bagpiper (below right) accompanies folk dancers.

LANGUAGE BUILDER

Valentin Vodnik also cared passionately about the voice of his native land. He was born in the Slovenian village of Šiške in 1758. At that time Austria ruled Slovenia and the Slovenian people were not allowed to speak their own language or teach it in the schools.

Then Napoleon won Slovenia from Austria. He let the people officially use Slovenian. Vodnik went to work. He wrote a Slovenian grammar book and many textbooks. He collected Slovenian proverbs, published a Slovenian calendar, and began work on a Slovenian dictionary.

But in the middle of his work, disaster fell. Austria took over Slovenia again. The Austrians would let Vodnik work only as a part-time teacher. His friends advised him to leave the country. But Vodnik could not separate himself from his beloved homeland. Instead he wandered the streets, poor and lonely. He died of a heart attack in 1819. But one day Slovenian literature would grow and flourish from the foundation he had laid.

MOTHER OF THOUSANDS

Agnes Gonxha Bojaxhui was born in 1910 to Albanian parents in the Macedonian city of Skopje. She loved her family, music, and trips to the mountains. But she loved God more. By the time she was twelve, Agnes knew she would become a nun. Nine years later she took her vows and the name that would become a symbol of love to the whole world—Teresa.

Teresa went to India and became first a teacher, then principal of a Catholic school in Calcutta. In 1946, she felt God had called her to serve the poorest of the poor. Two years later she left the

Mother Teresa receiving the 1979 Nobel Peace Prize

teaching nuns, took a course in hygiene, and moved to the slums of Calcutta. She began with five abandoned children, whom she taught in a public park.

Since then Teresa has cared for thousands of homeless, sick, and dying people. She is known the world over as Mother Teresa of Calcutta. She has received many awards, including the 1979 Nobel Peace Prize. But none of this matters as much to Mother Teresa as the fact that she is serving her God by caring for his poor.

YUGOSLAV'S HERO AND LEADER

Josip Broz Tito was born in 1892 in the Croatian village of Kumrovec. He had fourteen brothers and sisters, so his family had little money to spare. When he was fifteen, Tito went off to learn to be a locksmith. Then he took several jobs as a metalworker. Already he was interested in groups that tried to improve conditions for workers.

Young Pioneers is a youth organization. They are
trained to become future leaders in the Communist party.

In 1913 Tito was called to military service in the Austro-Hungarian army. When he refused to fight against his fellow Slavs, he was thrown in jail. Later he spoke up for the rights of prisoners of war and fought in the Russian Revolution. By the time he returned to Yugoslavia in 1920, he was ready to join her Communist party.

It was World War II, though, that made Tito a national hero. With determination and courage, he created, organized, and became head of the liberation army. This little group, known as the Partisans, did much to sabotage and weaken the German occupation of Yugoslavia.

Many wounded Partisans were brought to a base on Malta for treatment. While there, they were taught the use of both enemy and allied small arms by British instructors (left). Tito, leader of the Partisans, had his headquarters in a cave in the mountains (right).

When the war was over, it was obvious that Tito would become Yugoslavia's political leader. Under his leadership, Yugoslavia became an important voice for the countries that didn't want to take sides with either the East or the West.

Many people wondered what would happen to Yugoslavia after Tito. It was obvious no single leader could replace him. It was decided that nine people, known as the presidency, would take his place. When Tito died in 1980, Yugoslavia mourned him but continued down the path he had laid for her.

More and more Yugoslavs are now working in industry. A man is mining
marble (above) and below are workers in a pharmaceutical plant.

Chapter 7

EVERYDAY LIFE

REBUILDING

Before World War II, Yugoslavia had one of the poorest economies in Europe. More than three fourths of her people lived on small farms and worked with crude equipment. Few could read or write. Many died of disease or starvation. Groups of rich and middle-class people lived well in the cities. But they did little for their fellow countrymen, rural or urban.

Then came World War II and a civil war. Nearly two million Yugoslavs died and their country was devastated. Tito and his Communist party had a huge job ahead of them—rebuilding Yugoslavia. They began by seizing all industries and putting them under government ownership. Then they seized most of the farmlands and set up collective farms. Not everyone liked these methods, but there was little anyone could do to stop them.

Ironworks in Bosnia (left) and an offshore oil rig in the Adriatic Sea

THE RED-TAPE TRAP

The government soon found itself with an age-old problem—bureaucracy. There were so many officials and so much red tape that it was difficult to get anything done. So Yugoslavia began to "decentralize." Soon workers had most of the responsibility for running their industries. Each factory or other group of workers elected some of its own people to serve on a workers' council. The council elected a board of management. The board of management chose a trained director. If that director didn't perform well, he or she could be fired by the workers.

That is still basically how things are done in Yugoslavia. Private individuals *can* start businesses. But they have to borrow money from government-controlled banks. And the government restricts the size of private businesses.

 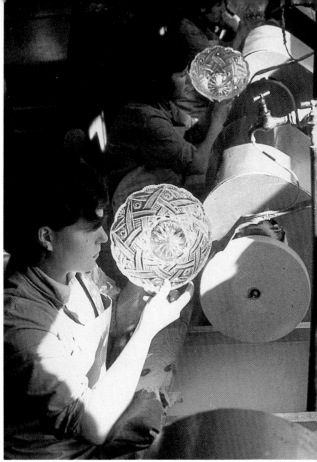

A thermoelectric power plant (left) and a crystal grinder at work

Some non-Communist tricks from the West have been introduced into Yugoslav business. Different firms compete fiercely with one another. Advertising lures people to buy the goods of one company or another. Credit ("buy now—pay later") is a firm part of the economy. Until recently it all seemed to be working and Yugoslavia, although facing an economic crisis in the early 1980s, had one of the more dynamic economies in eastern Europe.

More and more Yugoslav people are working in industry. They make automobiles and ships, chemicals and textiles, processed foods, flour, refined sugar, tobacco products, machinery, products of metal and wood, and many, many handcrafted items.

Vineyards planted in a gridwork of stone fences

THOSE STUBBORN FARMERS

Tito's early plans for farmers didn't work out so well, though. The farmers opposed collective farms. So the government allowed them to return to private farming. Most of them did. But the government also formed farm cooperatives to help with marketing, improvement loans, and new agricultural techniques.

Today Yugoslavia's leading agricultural products include corn, wheat, sugar beets, oats, barley, potatoes, tobacco, grapes and other fruit, olives, sheep, and cattle.

FRIENDS AND NEIGHBORS

Yugoslavia does most of her trading with countries in western Europe, such as Italy and West Germany. Her chief exports are livestock, machinery, plastics, metals, textiles, and forest products.

But Yugoslavia has to import more things than she exports. Her chief imports are crude oil, coal, motor vehicles, machinery, and textiles. Yugoslavia has figured out ways to lessen the problem of a deficit balance of trade (more imports than exports). First,

A Yugoslav family eating their main meal

tourists spend money in her beautiful vacation areas. Second, cargo ships earn money by carrying goods for other countries. Third, many Yugoslavs work in other countries and send money home. These three sources of income, plus what she earns on exports, help Yugoslavia pay for expensive imports, especially oil.

ORDINARY PEOPLE

About half of the Yugoslavs live in cities. They are housed in modern apartment buildings, older apartment buildings, or in older houses. European and other foreign automobiles, plus an Italian Fiat called a Fica that is made in Yugoslavia, are available.

Most people in the cities wear western clothing. Folk costumes are saved for special holidays. Restaurants serve delicious meals ending with little cakes and sweet, strong coffee.

Although the government owns radio and TV broadcasting, each republic has its own stations so residents can listen to some programs in their own language. They have to pay an owner's fee, though, to help finance those programs.

A house in the country

In the country, houses are made of brick, wood, or stone. Most of them have electricity—about 75 percent of rural families do now. Life today is easier than years ago in rural areas. But many young people dream about moving to the city someday. More and more Yugoslavs do that every year. But finding a place to live can be difficult.

NATIONAL COSTUMES

From raw materials, such as wool, hemp, linen, and leather, women make the traditional national costumes. These costumes vary from region to region.

In northern Slovenia the costumes are similar to the Tyrolean outfits worn by the Austrians. Tyrolean jackets and leather shorts are worn by the men, and the women wear dirndle dresses decorated with rich embroidery.

The women in southern Slovenia wear a bodice topped with a laced-up vest and a skirt and an apron. They wear leather belts decorated with ribbons and little chains and a cap or kerchief on their heads.

National costumes of Slovenia (left) and Croatia (right)

   Along the Adriadic coast the women usually wear a long, dark-colored smock with bright embroidery on the sleeves and front of the bodice. A short jacket is worn loose over this.

   Farther inland embroidered wool costumes are worn. Both men and women wear aprons, but the women's are embroidered. The men wear embossed leather belts. Some older men still wear bright knitted stockings and slippers called *opanci* (pumps).

   Embroidery dominates the costumes of Croatia. Women's costumes are often long white linen dresses. Over their dress, they wear a colored apron and a scarf over their shoulders. They usually wear a kerchief on their heads. Croatian men wear white shirts that hang loose at the waist topped by a colorful jacket. They wear high leather boots over linen trousers and small, round, brimless hats.

A bridal gown from Smilevo village in Macedonia (left).
Muslim costumes show the Turkish influence (right).

In Serbia the women also wear long white dresses covered with short aprons, but the aprons are decorated with beads, red embroidery, and silver thread. They wear jewelry around their necks and on their heads. On their heads they often wear a scarf that hangs down behind.

The Turkish influence can be seen in the baggy trousers, gathered at the ankles, worn by the Muslims in Bosnia-Hercegovina. They wear aprons with carpet-like patterns.

In Montenegro there are two kinds of costumes. There are the simple costumes of plain black and the rich costumes made of silk.

In Macedonia the costumes the men wear are short kilts showing the Greek influence.

In the large cities national costumes are worn only on special occasions, but out in the country the old traditional costumes can be seen frequently.

A 1934 watercolor by Ivan Generalić showing peasants rebelling against the police.

ENTERTAINMENT

Much of Yugoslav music is based on folk songs. But some of it sounds pretty modern. Yugoslavia has many fine orchestras and other performing groups.

The work of Yugoslav naive primitive, or untrained, painters is famous all over the world. Ivan Generalić is probably the best-known naive painter.

Everyone in Yugoslavia loves soccer. National teams have won many Olympic medals. Many cities have large stadiums that are used for soccer and track meets. There are other stadiums for basketball, handball, boxing, volleyball, tennis, and wrestling.

Cars traveling on a modern highway (left). A child has his own special seat on his father's bike.

In winter many Yugoslavs ski in the mountains of Slovenia and Bosnia. In summer they fish and swim in the Adriatic and mountain lakes.

For short trips in Yugoslavia, people ride bikes or motorcycles or drive their cars. For longer trips, they take buses. Trains also carry passengers in Yugoslavia. There are twelve international airports served by Yugoslavia's national airlines, JAT, and other international airlines.

FOLK DANCES

Costumes are particularly important as part of the various folk dances. Most dances are accompanied by a violin and sometimes an accordion and a flute are added. The only silent dance is one

On Sunday the people in the town of Cilipi wear their folk costumes.

done in Bosnia, which might stem from the fact that the Bosnians did not want to attract attention during their long years of foreign occupation.

RELIGION

Although Yugoslavia is a Communist country, there are churches throughout the land. There are also monasteries and mosques and even some synagogues. Religion is important to many people in Yugoslavia and they do belong to churches—and attend services. The largest group is Serbian Orthodox. But Roman Catholics predominate in Croatia and Slovenia. About 10 percent of the people are Muslims. They live in Bosnia, Macedonia, and southern Serbia. And there are Protestants, Jews, and other small religious groups, too.

The modern university center in Skopje

EDUCATION

Education is free from elementary school through the university level. Children are required to attend elementary schools from age seven to age fifteen. They have busy schedules and are expected to study hard. General secondary schools allow students to concentrate on social studies and linguistics or natural science and mathematics in four-year courses. Other four-year secondary schools are technical and vocational institutions.

There are approximately twenty universities in Yugoslavia. Advanced degrees can be earned in almost any subject. There also are art academies that offer training in music, drama, and the fine arts.

Adult education classes are held wherever possible to upgrade basic education and vocational training.

HEALTH AND SOCIAL SERVICES

All citizens are entitled to medical care. Workers are compensated for temporary absence from work, work disability, childbirth, and death. National health insurance covers the entire population of Yugoslavia and each republic or province is responsible for its program of health care.

Women are entitled to free health care during pregnancy, childbirth, and for six months after childbirth. Day nurseries are provided for young children.

Eighteen days paid vacation is the minimum per year for each worker and some receive more vacation days. Also, workers are eligible for pensions or financial coverage when they reach retirement age.

Intricately-carved wooden handicrafts for sale

HANDICRAFTS

Many weavers still produce fabric with embroidered decorations. Handmade lace can be found near the Italian coast and in Macedonia.

Some wonderful hand-thrown pottery is still made by skilled artisans in Croatia and Macedonia.

Different kinds of wall carpets can be found in Pirot in Serbia and Krusevo in Macedonia.

Rugs (left) and lace embroidery (right)

CRAFTS

Carved wooden objects used to be made by the shepherds, but today these objects are made by a wide variety of people. Pipes and musical instruments are decorated with ornamental carvings. Many pieces of furniture are carved with plant and floral designs.

Rugs are woven for use on floors, as wall hangings, or as bed coverings. Many of the rugs are made with ewes' wool; some are cropped short and others are long and shaggy; some are dyed and some are decorated with patterns.

Nineteenth century architecture in Ohrid

A SOVEREIGN STATE

Yugoslavia is a complex country, a combination of many languages, religions, ethnic groups, nationalities, and cultures. Her history is long and complicated, yet she has been a sovereign state for fewer than seventy years.

After World War II, under Tito's leadership, Yugoslavia became a representative voice for other countries, whatever their political persuasions, that didn't want to choose sides between the strict communism of the East and the free democracy of the West.

The people of Yugoslavia are strong and determined. They have lived through difficult times. They are proud of their nation and its accomplishments. They look to the future with a belief in themselves and in their unity.

The people of Yugoslavia are proud of their country and its accomplishments.

14° 16° 18° 20° 22°

1 2 3 4 5 6

A

Eferding · Linz · Pöggstall · Stockerau · Korneuburg · Hlohove · Banská Štiavnica · Málinec · Rimavská Sobota · Sátoraljaújhely · Sárospatak · Mukačevo
Ried · Wels · Enns · Grein · Krems · Tulln · Klosterneuburg · Vienna (Wien) · Trnava · Sered · CZECHOSLOVAKIA · Nitra · Lučenec · Ózd · Kazincbarcika · Tokaj · Nyíregyháza · Kisvárda · Beregovo
Gmunden · Sankt Pölten · Amstetten · Mödling · Schwechat · Bratislava · Vlčany · Levice · Balassagyarmat · Salgótarján · Miskolc · Hajdúnánás · Polgár · Mátészalka · Satu Ma
AUSTRIA · Waidhofen · Berndorf · Baden · Bruck · Kolárovo · Nové Zámky · Esztergom · Vác · Győrgyös · Heves · Mezőkövesd · Eger · Hajdúböszörmény · Carei

B

Bad Ischl · Mürzzuschlag · Neunkirchen · Wiener Neustadt · Sopron · Mosonmagyaróvár · Komárno · Komárom · Szentendre · Tata · Tatabánya · Bicske · Budapest · Jászberény · Vecsés · Debrecen · Simleu · Silvaniei
Rottenmann · Schladming · Bruck · Leoben · Kapfenberg · Kapuvár · Csorna · Győr · Mór · Érd · Ercsi · Monor · Cegléd · Nagykőrös · Szolnok · Karcag · Püspökladány · Betettyóújfalu · Derecske · Oradea · Zalá
Fohnsdorf · Knittelfeld · Eggenberg · Fürstenfeld · Szombathely · Sárvár · Kőszeg · Pápa · Veszprém · Székesfehérvár · Várpalota · Lajosmizse · Törökszentmiklós · Túrkeve · Mezőtúr · Dévaványa · Szarvas · Vésztő · Huedin
Murau · Judenburg · Voitsberg · Graz · Feldbach · Körmend · Zalaegerszeg · Keszthely · HUNGARY · Sárbogárd · Dunaújváros · Kecskemét · Kiskunfélegyháza · Kunszentmárton · Békés · Oroshaza · Beius
Friesach · Sankt Veit · Wolfsberg · Leibnitz · Maribor · Murska Sobota · Čakovec · Nagykanizsa · Dombóvár · Dunaföldvár · Szabadszállás · Kiskőrös · Csongrád · Szentes · Mezőtúr · Békéscsaba · Gyula
Villach · Klagenfurt · Dravograd · Ptuj · Varaždin · Koprivnica · Kaposvár · Tolna · Paks · Kalocsa · Kiskunhalas · Kiskunmajsa · Hódmezővásárhely · Makó · Battonya · Arad

C

TRIGLAV · Bled · Kranj · Celje · Križevci · Djurdjevac · Szekszárd · Komló · Bátaszék · Jánoshalma · Kiskundorozsma · Szeged · Tótkomlós · Curtici
Tolmin · Idrija · Škofja Loka · Ljubljana · Brežice · Bjelovar · Virovitica · Pécs · Mohács · Baja · Mélykút · Battonya · Nădlac · CURCUBATA 6,063 FT · RO
Gorizia · Cerknica · Krško · Zagreb · Ivanić Grad · Kutina · Garešnica · Daruvar · Siklós · Bačka · Senta · Kikinda · Lipova · Brad
Monfalcone · Postojna · Kočevje · Crnomelj · Sisak · Lipik · Slavonska · Požega · Našice · Apatin · Osijek · Bajmok · Sombor · Topola · Mol · Ada · Timișoara · Lugoj · Hunedoara · Deva
Trieste · Piran · Buzet · Rijeka (Fiume) · Sušak · Ogulin · Petrinja · Bosanska Gradiška · Djakovo · Vukovar · Vinkovci · Kula · Vrbas · Bečej · Jimbolia · Reșița · Caransebeș · Hațeg
Poreč · ISTRIAN PEN. · Bakar · Crikvenica · Slunj · Bosanska Kostajnica · Bosanska Novi · Derventa · Bosanski Samac · Srbobran · Bačka Palanka · Čurug · Novi Sad · Zrenjanin (Petrovgrad) · Vršac · Bela Crkva · Anina · Oravița · Bozovici · Petroșa · Lupeni
Rovinj · Pula · KRK · Punat · Brinje · Prijedor · Bosanska Dubica · Bosanska Gradiška · Bosanski Samac · Sremski Karlovci · Ruma · Sremska Mitrovica · Pančevo · Belgrade (Beograd) · Orsova · IRON GATE · Drobeta Turnu-Severin · Strehaia
KAMENJAK · CRES · RAB · Otočac · Gospić · Banja Luka · Kotor Varoš · Gradačac · Brčko · Bijeljina · Šabac · Smederevo · Požarevac · Negotin · Bregovo · Novo-Sel
UNIJE · SUSAK · Karlobag · PAG · Bosanski Petrovac · Ključ · Tešanj · Maglaj · Doboj · Gračanica · Tuzla · Loznica · Valjevo · Rača · Svilajnac · Bor · Vidin
MOLAT · Novigrad · Zadar · Benkovac · Skradin · Gračac · Knin · Donji Vakuf · Travnik · Zenica · Vareš · Vlasenica · Zvornik · Gornji Milanovac · Bă
DUGI · Šibenik · Livno · Glamoč · Bugojno · Visoko · Titovo Užice · Čačak · Kragujevac · Zaječar · Kula · Gramada · Vidin
KORNAT · Trogir · Sinj · Duvno · Prozor · Sarajevo · Rogatica · Višegrad · Kraljevo · Vitanovac · Paraćin · Bor · Vălče

D

YUGOSLAVIA
Split · BRAČ · Makarska · Imotski · Mostar · Nevesinje · Foča · Cajniče · Priboj · Nova Varos · Raška · Trstenik · Kruševac · Aleksinac · Niš · Pirot · Mikhaylovgra · Berko
Vis · VIS · HVAR · Ljubuški · Domanovići · Stolac · Gacko · Pljevlja · Prijepolje · Sjenica · Prokuplje · Leskovac · Dimitrovgra
BIŠEVO · ŠOLTA · Blato · KORČULA · Metković · Bileća · DURMITOR 8,274 FT · Bijelo Polje · Novi Pazar · Kuršumlija · Vlasotince · Breznik · Sof
LASTOVO · MLJET · Gruž · Trebinje · Nikšić · Ivangrad · Kosovska Mitrovica · Priština · Trǔn · Radomir
PELAGRUŽA (YUGO.) · Dubrovnik · Danilovgrad · Kotor · Titograd · Djakovica · Prizren · Gnjilane · Vranje · Kriva Palanka · Kyustendil · Bohov Dol
Pescara · Ortona · Cetinje · Virpazar · Gusinje · Peć · DJARAVICA 8,714 FT · Kumanovo · Kratovo (Gorna Dz · Blago
Lanciano · Vasto · Termoli · Bar · Shkodra · Puka · Kukësi · Tetovo · Skopje · Kočani · Štip

E

Agnone · Larino · Torremaggiore · Vieste · Lezha · Peshkopia · KORAB 9,026 FT · Gostivar · Titov Veles · Radoviš · Pehčevo
Campobasso · San Marco · Monte Sant'Angelo · Manfredonia · Kruja · Klosi · Maqellara · Kičevo · Debar · Strumica
Caserta · Lucera · San Severo · Foggia · Bulqiza · Struga · Ohrid · Demir Kapia · Prilep
Naples (Napoli) · Avellino · Cerignola · Barletta · Trani · Bisceglie · Molfetta · Bari · Durrësi · Tirana · Kruševo · Bitola
Aversa · Benevento · Ariano Irpino · Canosa · Andria · Ruvo · Bitonto · Mola · Monopoli · Kavaja · Peqini · Elbasani · Stalin · Edhessa · Kilki
Torre Annunziata · Avigliano · Corato · Altamura · Gioia del Colle · Fasano · Cerriku · Lushnja · Gramshi · Florina · Náousa · Langa
Sorrento · Eboli · Melfi · Spinazzola · Gravina · Matera · Ginosa · Ostuni · Ceglie Messapico · Brindisi · Fieri · Berati · Patosi · Korça · Ptolemais · Veroia
Agropoli · Sala Consilina · Potenza · Massafra · Taranto · Pisticci · Grottaglie · Francavilla Fontana · Mesagne · SAZANI · Vlora · Stalin

Longitude East of Greenwich

48° 46° 44° 42°

MINI-FACTS AT A GLANCE

GENERAL INFORMATION

Official Name: Socialist Federal Republic of Yugoslavia

Capital: Belgrade

Official Languages: Serbo-Croatian, Slovenian, and Macedonian

Other Languages: Hungarian, Italian, and Albanian

Government: Yugoslavia is officially a socialist federal republic including the separate republics of Serbia, Croatia, Macedonia, Montenegro, Slovenia, and Bosnia-Hercegovina, as well as the autonomous Serbian provinces of Kosovo-Metohija and Vojvodina. There is no longer one president since the death of Marshal Tito in 1980. Instead, there is a nine-member presidency including one representative from each republic and autonomous province. Each member of the presidency or council takes turns serving as president of the council and head of state for one year.

There is a two-house legislature called the Federal Assembly. One house is called the Federal Chamber; it has 220 members. The other, called the Chamber of Republics and Autonomous Provinces, has 88 members. In addition to acting as a legislature, the Federal Assembly elects members of the cabinet who administer the departments of the national government. The cabinet itself is called the Federal Executive Council. The president of the council is the premier.

Each republic and province has a government of its own modeled after the national government. At the local level, republics and provinces are divided into 508 communes, each of which has an assembly and a communal council.

Flag: The national flag has three stripes, colored blue, white, and red. A red star in the center symbolizes communism.

Coat of Arms: The Yugoslavian coat of arms has a torch for each of the nation's six republics. The date on it, 1943, is the year that communism was born in Yugoslavia.

National Song: "Hej Sloveni" ("Hey Slavs")

Religion: Roman Catholic (approximately 30 percent); Serbian and Macedonian Orthodox (35 percent); Sunni Muslim (12 percent)

Money: The basic unit of money in Yugoslavia is the dinar, which is equal to 100 para. The exchange rate as of October, 1982, was 52.84 new dinars to one United States dollar and in October, 1983, the rate of exchange was 111 new dinars to one U.S. dollar.

Weights and Measures: Yugoslavians use the metric system.

Population: 22,352,162 (1981 census)

Cities:

Belgrade (capital of Serbia) 1,455,064
Zagreb (capital of Croatia) 1,168,567
Skopje (capital of Macedonia) 503,449
Sarajevo (capital of Bosnia-Hercegovina) 447,687
Ljubljana (capital of Slovenia) 303,469
Novi Sad (capital of Vojvodina) 213,860
Priština (capital of Kosovo-Metohija) 211,156
Titograd (capital of Montenegro) 132,086

(Population figures as of March 31, 1981)

GEOGRAPHY

Highest Point: Mount Triglav, 9,393 ft. (2,863 m)

Lowest Point: Sea level

Coastline: 490 mi. (788 km) along the Adriatic Sea

Rivers: Longest river in Yugoslavia is the Sava, 584 mi. (940 km)

Lakes: Lake Scutari in Montenegro is Yugoslavia's largest lake.

Mountains: Much of Yugoslavia is mountainous and part of the Alps run through the country.

Climate: Yugoslavia's climate is extremely varied. The northeastern plains have a continental climate (hot summers and cold winters). In the continental areas, the average temperature in winter is 30° F. (-1° C) and in summer it is between 75° and 80° F. (24-27° C). The Adriatic coast has warm winters and hot summers. Sometimes the temperature goes up to 100° F. (38° C). Temperatures in the mountains are usually lower than along the coast or on the plains. In the Alps, winters are cold and summers are short and cool.

In the Pannonian Plains the summer temperature is often 100° F. (38° C), but in winter the winds come in from the north, plunging temperatures into the 30s (-1 C). On the other hand, parts of Macedonia have a subtropical climate.

Rainfall in Yugoslavia is as varied as the temperatures. Not far from the coastal region, which has much sunshine, is one of the wettest spots in Europe. In Montenegro's Dinaric Alps, the average annual rainfall is over 16 ft. (5 m).

Greatest Distances: North to south—415 mi. (668 km)
East to west—475 mi. (764 km)

Area: 98,766 sq. mi. (255,804 km²).

NATURE

Trees: Forests cover 35 percent of the land. Oak, beech, chestnut, and evergreens grow in many mountainous areas. Olive trees have grown in the Coastal Region since the days of the Greeks.

Fish: The Adriatic Sea yields more than 350 kinds of fish.

Animals: Animal life is similar to that in other countries in eastern and central Europe. There are still deer, wild pigs, wolves, foxes, bears, lynx, and wildcats in the mountains; chamois and alpine rabbits are in the highest areas. In the karst region there are many rare species, including the blind salamander, and venomous snakes. Along the coast there are Mediterranean species such as lizards and insects that can live during dry, hot summers.

EVERYDAY LIFE

Food: Because Yugoslavia is made up of many different ethnic groups, the food is varied in different parts of the country. In Serbia, chicken soup, grilled meats, and a spicy meatball dish called *čevapčiči* are popular. In Macedonia, lamb dishes are favorites; in Slovenia, sausages are common. Along the coast seafood dishes such as deep-fried squid are served. As for beverages, Yugoslavs like wine and Turkish coffee, but a plum brandy called *slivovitz* has the distinction of being the national drink.

Housing: There are different kinds of housing in different parts of the country. In Slovenia, houses reflect European architecture of a century ago. In Bosnia, the Muslim influence is seen. At present, there is a housing shortage, mostly because of a shortage of building materials, rising construction costs, and expanding urban areas. For the migrants from the rural areas to the cities, the problem of finding adequate housing is great. Single adult males often live in dormitories because they can't get apartments.

Holidays:
January 1-2, New Year
May 1-2, Labor Days
July 4, Fighters' Day
November 29-30, Republic Days

Some Major Events in Each Republic:

Serbia

End of March/beginning of April	International Motor Show, Belgrade
May	"Belgrade Spring," song festival, Belgrade
May	"Themes from Homolje," folk art, Kučevo
May	International Textile Fair, Leskovac
May	International Agricultural Show, Novi Sad
May 25	Youth Day, Belgrade
End of May	Narcissus Festival, Divčibare
End of July	Harvest Festival, Subotica
July-September	Folk Concerts, Belgrade
Beginning of August	Danube Regatta, Novi Sad, Belgrade and Smederevo
End of August/beginning of September	Film Festival, Niš
End of August/beginning of September	International Equestrian Games, Požarevac and Ljubičevo

September	International Theater Festival, Belgrade
September	Festival of Folk Music, Belgrade
Beginning of October	International Festival of Children's Folk Songs and Dances, Belgrade
Beginning of October	Autumn Fair, Novi Sad
October	International Musical Festival, Belgrade
October	October Salon (art show), Belgrade
End of October	International Book Fair, Belgrade

Slovenia

April	Alpe-Adria International Trade Fair, Ljubljana
Mid May-September	Concerts, Folk Displays, and Fashion, Sporting, and Cultural Events on the coast, Portorož and Piran
May-October	Summer Program of Concerts and Folk Displays, Bled
Beginning of June	International Riding Tournament, Lipica
Mid June	Folk Festivals with International Groups, Koper, Portorož, Izola, Piran, and Ankaran
July-August	Folk Evenings, Bled
July-August	Cultural Events, Ljubljana
Beginning of August	Song Festival, Portorož
Mid August	International Trade Fair of Upper Carniola, Kranj
End of August/beginning of September	International Wine Fair, Ljubljana
Mid September	Flower Show, Ljubljana
November	International Ski Expo Fair, Ljubljana

Bosnia-Hercegovina

End of March/beginning of April	Yugoslav Song Festival, Sarajevo
Beginning of June	International Festival of Military Music, Sarajevo
Mid July	Festival of Yugoslav Folksongs, Ilidž
July 27	Jumping into the Neratva from the Old Bridge, Mostar
October	Slivovitz and Wine Fair, Sarajevo

Croatia

End of April	International Spring Fair and Tourism Congress, Zagreb
Second half of June	Song Festival, Istria and the Coastal Region
Mid June-mid August	Drama, Opera, Ballet, Concerts, and Folk Displays, Split
June-August	Folk Displays and Concerts, Pula
Beginning of July	Festival of Light, Split
End of July	Folk Festival, Zagreb
July 27	Moreska (sword dance), Korčula
July-September	Open-air Performances, Opatija
July-September	Music, Drama, Folk Singing and Dancing, Zagreb
End of July-beginning of August	Festival of Yugoslav Feature Film, Pula
August 5	Historic Spear-throwing Contest on Horseback, Sinj
Beginning of September	Festival of Songs in the Kaj Dialect, Krapina
Mid September	International Autumn Trade Fair, Zagreb
December 29-30	Underwater Fishing Championships, Mali Lošinj

Macedonia

Beginning of May	Festival of Music, Folk Singing and Dancing of the Old Town, Ohrid
May	Evenings of Opera, Skopje
June	Skopje Trade Fair, Skopje
Beginning of July	Folk Events, Galičnik
Beginning of July	Festival of Balkan Folk Singing and Dancing, Ohrid
End of July	Folk Singing and Dancing, Bitola
July-August	Cultural and Tourist Events, Ohrid
End of August	Festival of Music and Folk Display in the Old Town, Ohrid
End of August	Poetry Readings, Struga
End of September	International Tobacco and Machinery Fair, Skopje

Montenegro

Beginning of June	Music Festivals, Budva and Sveti Stefan
End of June-September	Open-air Concerts and Theatrical Performances, Herceg-Novi

Culture: Yugoslavian culture today is complex. It is a mixture of old and new, folk tradition and communism, regional and national elements.

The country has a long theatrical tradition, going back to plays performed by monks in the Middle Ages. There are sixty professional theaters in Yugoslavia and over thirty children's theaters. The national theater in Belgrade has been in existence since 1868. It has its own opera, drama, and ballet companies.

Literature is also flourishing in Yugoslavia. Since 1950, because of fewer government restrictions, writers are freer to write what they choose than during the earliest days of communism. Many important novels since World War II have the war as their theme, including Dobrica Ćosić's *Daleko je sunce (Far Away Is the Sun)*, and Oskar Davico's *Pesma (The Poem)*, a story of youth during World War II. In 1961, Ivo Andrić won the Nobel Prize in literature. He is best known for *Na Drini ćuprija (The Bridge on the Drina)*, written in 1945.

Yugoslavian filmmakers are internationally famous. About 50 feature films and 150 shorts are made in Yugoslavia each year. Dušan Makavejev of Novi Sad is known around the world for *An Affair of the Heart* and *WR—Mysteries of the Organism.*

Folk arts are very important in Yugoslavia. Modern painting often has rural life as its theme. Folk dancing remains popular in rural Yugoslavia. Such folk arts as lace embroidery, carpet making, leatherwork, and pottery are widespread.

Sports and Recreation: Sports are very popular in Yugoslavia, especially soccer. Professional soccer games usually draw large crowds. Water polo and basketball are also popular. In the winter, many people ski in the mountains. In the summer, they fish and swim in the Adriatic.

Communications: Since 1956 the Yugoslav press has been able to operate relatively free of restrictions from the government.

There are twenty-nine daily newspapers published in Yugoslavia, printed in Serbian (Cyrillic alphabet), Croatian (Roman), Slovene, Macedonian, Hungarian, Italian, and Albanian. *Borba*, the Communist party paper, and the chief daily, *Politike*, both issued in Belgrade, express the official viewpoint.

Yugoslav radio and television are generally considered more interesting than similar broadcasts in other eastern European countries. Although the government controls radio and TV, each republic has its own stations that broadcast programs in many different languages, depending on the area. Programs are heard in such diverse languages as English, French, Albanian, and Spanish, as well as the native languages. Citizens pay an owners' fee to help finance programs.

Transportation: Building roads and railroads has been difficult in Yugoslavia because of the mountainous terrain. By the 1970s, though, the railroad system, expanded and improved, provided about 80 percent of public transportation. Many of Yugoslavia's railroads are run by electricity. In 1976, a new rail line was opened between Belgrade and the port of Bar on the Adriatic almost 300 mi. (483 km) away. In 1980, total miles of track was 6,413 mi. (10,319 km), 2,672 mi. (4,300 km) of which is electrified.

A new railway between Rijeka and Zagreb should be opened by 1990. Eventually, it will extend from Zagreb to the Hungarian border.

In recent years, road and air traffic has been expanding at a faster rate than railroad traffic. In 1980, there were 72,181 mi. (116,140 km) of roads.

Water transportation is also very important in Yugoslavia. There are several navigable rivers, including the Danube which has Novi Sad and Belgrade as its chief ports. Chief ports on the Adriatic are Rijeka, Koper, Split, Kardeljevo, Bar, and Dubrovnik.

The state airline, Jugoslovenski Aerotransport (JAT), provides domestic and international service. Flights run regularly from New York and Chicago to Belgrade, Lujbljana, and Zagreb. Also, there are flights from many European cities to Belgrade, with some serving Zagreb, as well as certain vacation spots in summer.

Schools: All Yugoslavian children between the ages of seven (six in Croatia) and fifteen must attend school. At the high school, or secondary, level, several kinds of training are available. But most students choose vocational or technical schools. Another alternative is a four-year gymnasium program that prepares students for college. Art schools and teacher-training schools train high-school-aged students to be teachers. After secondary school, for those who attend technical schools, there are two-year post-secondary schools.

There are about twenty universities in Yugoslavia, as well as advanced training programs for teachers. Some universities are very old. The largest, the University of Belgrade, was founded in 1863. The university at Ljubljana was founded in 1595 and the one in Zagreb in 1669.

Health: Health care has improved drastically since World War II. In the 1930s and 1940s, typhus, typhoid, and dysentery were common. Yugoslavia also had Europe's highest death rate from tuberculosis because of poor nutrition and sanitation. Now all that is changed. By the late 1970s, those diseases were very rare.

Health care is considered a right. A health care insurance program covers almost everyone. At the same time, health care in rural areas is not as good as in cities because most doctors want to practice medicine in the cities.

ECONOMY AND INDUSTRY

Principal Products:
Agriculture: Corn, livestock, potatoes, sugar beets, wheat, and tobacco

Manufacturing: Automobiles, chemicals, food products, machinery, metal products, textiles, and wood products.
Minerals: Iron, bauxite, chromite, coal, copper, lead, zinc, silver, gold, bismuth, cadmium, antimony, uranium, mercury, platinum, magnesium, nickel, cobalt, tin, asbestos, pyrites, graphite, gypsum, salt, talc, quartz, marble, asphalt, natural gas, and petroleum

IMPORTANT DATES

168 B.C. — Dalmatia, Macedonia, and most of Illyria become Roman provinces

A.D. 9 — Rome creates province of Illyricum (contemporary Yugoslavia without northern Serbia)

A.D. 300s — Gothic, Hunic, and Avaric invaders sweep through the region

395 — Roman Empire is split in two; line of division runs through Balkans

602 — Slavs invade the Balkans

Croatia

500s-600s — Croatian tribes migrate from the Ukraine into land between the Sava and Drava rivers

800s — Northern Croats come under control of the Franks and the Dalmatian Croats come under control of the Eastern Empire.

900s — Croats begin to develop a sense of identity

910-1102 — Croatia becomes a free and independent kingdom

1102 — Croatia becomes part of Hungary

1463 — Bosnia falls to Turks

1526 — Hungary falls to Turks and with it, Croatia

1527 — Croatian nobles submit to Hapsburg Emperor Ferdinand, who also becomes ruler of Hungary

late 1500s — Turks absorb much of Croatia and almost all of Slovenia

1573 — Peasant rebellion led by Matija Gubec

1699 — Hapsburgs get all of Croatia and Slovenia back from Turks

1841 — Bishop Josip Juraj Strossmayer founds the National party

1867 — Strossmayer founds the Yugoslav Academy of Zagreb

1870—First Yugoslav Congress held in Slovenia

Serbia

late 800s—Byzantine monks Methodius and Cyril convert Serbs to Christianity and introduce Byzantine culture into area

1168—Stefan Nemanjić becomes ruler of a tract of land that eventually becomes Serbia

1219—Sava becomes first Serbian archbishop

1331-35—Serbian Empire reaches its zenith under Tsar Stephen Dušan

1349—Dušan introduces legal code known as Dušanov Zakonik

1389—Turks defeat Serbian armies in Kosovo

1459—Smederevo falls to Turks; fall of Serbian state

1463—Bosnia falls to Turks

1482—Hercegovina falls to Turks

1499—Montenegro falls to Turks

1521—Belgrade falls to Turks

1557—Serbian church allowed to have its own patriarchate

1766—Serbian church's patriarchate abolished

1804—Serbian uprising led by Karadjordje

1813—Serbs defeated

1815—Second Serbian revolt

1830—Serbia becomes autonomous

1867—Turkish garrisons evacuate fortresses in Serbia

1878—Treaty of Berlin; Serbia becomes independent

1912-13—Balkan Wars

Dalmatia

(Dalmatia, now part of the republic of Croatia, was closely associated with Croatia throughout its history)

1200s-1700s — Venetians rule Dalmatia

1806-13 — Napoleon occupies the province

1815 — Dalmatia given to Austria, which rules it until 1918

Slovenia

500s — Slavs first come to Slovenia

700s — German rulers take over Slovenia

1500s — Slovenia becomes part of the Austrian Empire; remains so until 1918

Bosnia-Hercegovina

late 1100s — Bosnia becomes an independent state

1463 — Bosnia conquered by Turks

1482 — Hercegovina falls to the Turks

Montenegro

1499 — Montenegro falls to Turks

late 1600s — Njegoš family becomes ruling clan

1851 — Offices of prince and bishop separated

1878 — Montenegro recognized as an independent princedom

Macedonia

400s-500s — Slavs arrive

893-927 — Most of Macedonia conquered by the first Bulgarian Empire

1300s — Macedonia conquered by Serbia; Macedonia falls to the Turks; remains a Turkish province until 1900s

Yugoslavia

1914 — Austria's Archduke Francis Ferdinand is assassinated

1915 — Serbian army retreats to Montenegro and Albania

1918 — World War I ends; King Petar I of Serbia proclaimed king of Yugoslavia, a constitutional monarchy

1921 — Alexander becomes king

1929 — Alexander becomes dictator

1934 — Alexander murdered by Croatian terrorists

1939 — World War II begins

1941 — Yugoslav government becomes an ally of the Axis; Prince Paul deposed; Yugoslavia taken over by the Nazis and Fascists

1944 — Tito's Partisans and the Russian army drive the Nazis from Belgrade

1945 — Tito elected head of state

1946 — Communist constitution becomes law

1948 — Tito breaks with the Soviet Union

1974 — Presidency established

1980 — Tito dies

1984 — XIV Olympic Winter Games held in Sarajevo

STATESMEN OF YUGOSLAVIA

Bosnia and Hercegovina
Bosnia and Hercegovina was occupied by Austria in 1878

1878	Governor Freiherr Josef von Philippovich Philippsberg (1819-89)
1878-81	Governor Wilhelm Nikolaus, Herzog von Württemberg (1828-96)
1881-82	Governor Freiherr Hermann Dahlen-Orlaburg (1828-87)
1882-1903	Governor Freiherr Johann von Appel (1826-1906)
1903-07	Governor Freiherr Eugen von Albori (1838-1915)
1907-09	Governor Freiherr Anton von Winzor (1844-1910)

Bosnia and Hercegovina was annexed by Austria-Hungary in 1908

1909-11	Governor Freiherr Marian von Varesanin-Vares (1847-1917)
1911-14	Governor Oskar Potiorek (1853-1933)
1915-18	Governor Freiherr Stefan von Sarkotic-Lovcen (1858-1939)

Bosnia and Hercegovina became part of Yugoslavia in 1918

Croatia
Croatia was ruled by Hungary from 1091; Turkey from 1526; part of France from 1809-1913; and Austria-Hungary until 1918. In 1918 Croatia became part of Yugoslavia and in 1941 it declared independence.

1941-44	Dictator Ante Pavelich (1889-1959)

1941-43   King Aimone of Spoleto (kingdom created by the Italians)

Croatia was then under German rule until it was reunited with Yugoslavia after World War II.

Montenegro

Montenegro was independent from the fourteenth century, but little is known about the early rulers.

1697-1737   Prince-Bishop Danilo Petrović (1677-1737)

1737-   Prince-Bishop Sava (-1782)

   -1766   Prince-Bishop Vasisi (-1766)

1766-74   Prince-Bishop Stephen the Little (-murdered 1774)

1774-82   Prince-Bishop Sava

1782-1830   Prince-Bishop Petar I, nephew of Sava (1760?-1830)

1830-51   Prince-Bishop Petar II, nephew of Petar I (1812-51)

1851-60   Lord Danilo II (1826-assassinated 1860)

1860-1910   Prince Nicholas I, nephew of Danilo II (1841-1921)

1910-18   King Nicholas I, abdicated 1918

Montenegro was occupied by Austria from 1916-18 and in 1918 it became part of Yugoslavia.

Serbia

Serbia was ruled by Turkey from 1459-1829.

1804-13   National Leader Karadjordje (George Petrović) (1766?-1817)

1817-39   Prince Miloš Obrenović (1780-1860)

1839   Prince Milan, son of Miloš Obrenović (1819-39)

1839-42   Prince Michael, son of Miloš Obrenović (1823-assassinated 1868)

1842-58   Prince Alexander Karadjordjević, son of Karadjordje (1806-85)

1858-60   Prince Miloš Obrenović

1860-68   Prince Michael, son of Miloš Obrenović

1868-82   Prince Milan, grandnephew of Milos Obrenović (1854-1901)

In 1882 Prince Milan took the title of king.

1882-89   King Milan I, abdicated 1889

1889-1903   King Alexander I, son of Milan I (1876-assassinated 1903)

1903-21   King Petar I Karadjordjević, son of Alexander (1844-1921)

Serbia was occupied by Austria from 1915-18. In 1918 it became part of Yugoslavia

Yugoslavia

Yugoslavia was declared a kingdom on December 1, 1918.

1919-21   King Petar I (of Serbia) (1844-1921)

1918-21   Regent Alexander, son of Petar I (1888-assassinated 1934)

In 1921 Alexander became Alexander I, king of the Serbs, Croats, and Slovenes.

1921-34   King Alexander I

The thirteenth century church of St. John Caneo overlooks Lake Ohrid.

1934-41   Regent Paul, cousin of Alexander I (1893-1976)

1934-45   King Petar II, son of Alexander I (1923-   )

In 1945 Yugoslavia became a communist nation.

1945-53   President Ivan Ribar (1881-   )

1953-1980   President Josip Broz Tito (1892-1980)

1912-26   Prime Minister Nikola Pašić (1846-1926)

1945-63   President of Federal Executive Council Josip Broz Tito

1963-   President of Federal Executive Council Petar Stambolić (1912-   )

IMPORTANT PEOPLE

Ivo Andrić (1892-1975), historical novelist, won Nobel Prize in literature in 1961

Agnes Gonxha Bojaxhui (Mother Teresa) (1910-   ), Catholic nun, winner of the Nobel Peace Prize

Miodrag Bulatović (1913-   ), contemporary writer, wrote *The Red Cockerel*

Dragiša Cvetković (1893-   ), premier in early World War II, signed the Tripartite Pact with Germany and its allies in 1941

Saint Cyril (c. 827-69), apostle to the Slavs

Oskar Davičo (1909-   ), novelist, writer of *Pesma (The Poem)*

Goce Delčev (1872-1906), Macedonian revolutionary

Milovan Djilas (1911-   ), political leader close to Tito during World War II and after, later fell out of favor with the government and sentenced to prison

Stephen Dušan (1308-55), emperor of Serbia, the last of the Nemanjić family

Ilija Garašanin (1812-74), leading Serbian statesman, 1842-67, author of
  Naćertanije (1844)

Damian Gruev (1871-1906), Macedonian revolutionary, worked closely with
  Goce Delčev

Ljubo Ivančić (1921-   ), contemporary Yugoslav painter

Karadjordje (Djordje Petrović, "Black George") (1766?-1817), leader of the
  Serbian revolt of 1804, founder of Karadjordjević dynasty of Serbia

Alexander Karadjordjević (1888-1934), son of Petar I, king of Serbia and later
  king of Yugoslavia and dictator

Petar Karadjordjević (Petar I) (1844-1921), king of Yugoslavia

Petar Karadjordjević (Petar II) (1923-   ), last king of Yugoslavia

Paul Karadjordjević (1893-   ), cousin of King Alexander, after whose death
  he became regent for King Petar II, forced into exile in 1941

Prince Lazar (1329-89) led Serbs, Bosnians, Albanians, etc., against the Turks

Saint Methodius (825-84), brother of Saint Cyril and bishop of Smyrna in
  Pannonia

Ivan Meštrović (1883-1962), Croatian sculptor and nationalist

Draža Mihailovic (1893-1946), Serbian army officer, leader of the Chetniks who
  opposed the Germans, but who supported King Petar's government, tried and
  executed by Tito's regime

Stefan Mokranjac (1856-1914), composer of choral music inspired by Serbian
  folk songs

Nemanjić family (1168-1371), rulers of independent medieval Serbian state

Danilo Petrović Njegoš (1670-1725), orthodox bishop of Montenegro and ruler,
  fought the Turks

Petar (II) Njegoš (1813-51), Prince-bishop of Montenegro, poet

Miloš Obrenović (1780-1860), founder of Obrenović dynasty, first prince ruler of
  autonomous Serbia

Gavrilo Princip (1895-1918), assassin of Archduke Francis Ferdinand

Stefan Radić (1871-1928), with his brother Antun founded the Croat Peasant
  party

Josip Broz Tito (1892-1980), leader of the Communist republic of Yugoslavia for
  almost forty years

Valentin Vodnik (1758-1819), author of Slovenian grammar book and textbooks
  and champion of the Slovenian language

Many Yugoslavs ski in the mountains. In 1984 Yugoslavia was host to the fourteenth Winter Olympic Games.

INDEX

Page numbers that appear in boldface type indicate illustrations

About the Author

Carol Greene has a B.A. in English Literature from Park College, Parkville, Missouri and an M.A. in Musicology from Indiana University, Bloomington. She's worked with international exchange programs, taught music and writing, and edited children's books. She now works as a freelance writer in St. Louis, Missouri and has had published over 20 books for children and a few for adults. When she isn't writing, Ms. Greene likes to read, travel, sing, and do volunteer work at her church. She has written over twenty books for Childrens Press, including *England* in the Enchantment of the World series.